COVID-19 STORIES FROM THE SWEDISH WELFARE STATE

The Pandemicracy

Barbara Czarniawska, Josef Pallas and Elena Raviola

First published in Great Britain in 2025 by

Bristol University Press
University of Bristol
1–9 Old Park Hill
Bristol
BS2 8BB
UK
t: +44 (0)117 374 6645
e: bup-info@bristol.ac.uk

Details of international sales and distribution partners are available at bristoluniversitypress.co.uk

British Library Cataloguing in Publication Data
A catalogue record for this book is available from the British Library

ISBN 978-1-5292-4312-3 hardcover
ISBN 978-1-5292-4313-0 ePub
ISBN 978-1-5292-4314-7 ePdf

Cover design: Lyn Davies Design
Front cover image: Stocksy/SIYUN YUH
Bristol University Press uses environmentally responsible print partners.
Printed and bound in Great Britain by CPI Group (UK) Ltd, Croydon, CR0 4YY

FSC
www.fsc.org
MIX
Paper | Supporting responsible forestry
FSC® C013604

In Memory of Barbara Czarniawska

Transforming our book into its English version has been a deeply moving and challenging process, made particularly poignant by the loss of our dear friend and colleague, Barbara Czarniawska, who passed away on 7 April 2024 after battling a prolonged illness. More than just a pivotal figure in our professional project, Barbara was a cherished part of our lives, enriching our academic and personal worlds alike.

Barbara's impact on academic research spans wide and deep. A trailblazer in organizational theory within the field of organization and management studies, her innovative thinking has profoundly influenced scholarly dialogue across the globe. She skilfully wove narrative structures into organizational studies, providing transformative insights that melded sociological views with rigorous field research. Her major works, including various seminal books and articles, have reshaped our understanding of organizations, not merely as business ventures but as complex socio-political entities that articulate their roles and effectiveness within society.

But Barbara's scholarly endeavours reached far beyond her primary discipline. Her research made significant inroads into sociology, political science, science and technology studies, media and communication studies and literary studies. In each area, she introduced novel perspectives and cross-disciplinary methodologies that enhanced scholarly understanding and challenged academic norms.

Barbara was known for her forward-thinking, insightful and at times provocative stances, which inspired scholars to engage in critical and creative thinking. She was a pioneer of innovative qualitative research methods, particularly in analysing the intricate dynamics of organizational behaviour, leaving a lasting impact on numerous researchers and students. Barbara's true legacy, however, lies not only in her scholarly publications but also in her role as a mentor. She shared her relentless curiosity and meticulous attention to detail with everyone who had the privilege to learn from her.

It has truly been an honour and a privilege to have had Barbara in our lives, sharing her lengthy and enriching journey with us. Her intellectual and personal contributions will continue to inspire and resonate within us and the rest of our academic community and beyond for many years to come. Thank you, Barbara, for your incredible generosity and dedication, and for the lasting mark you've left on all of us.

Elena Raviola and Josef Pallas
Gothenburg and Uppsala
April 2024

Contents

List of Figures and Tables

Figures

Tables

About the Authors

Barbara Czarniawska was Professor Emerita at the Gothenburg Research Institute, University of Gothenburg. She took a feminist and processual perspective on organizing and recently explored links between popular culture and management practice, the future of the welfare state and the robotization of work. She was interested in fieldwork techniques and in the application of narratology (the study of storytelling) to social science studies.

Josef Pallas is Professor of Management and Organization at the Department of Business Studies, Uppsala University. His research focuses on the organization and governance of public sector organizations in general and universities, state authorities and municipalities in particular. He is interested in the interplay between governance ideas related to audit and evaluation, media and news production, communication and issues related to professionalism and collegiality.

Elena Raviola is Torsten and Wanja Söderberg Professor of Design Management at the Academy of Art and Design, University of Gothenburg, and runs the Business and Design Lab research centre at the same university. Her research examines how digitalization and automation are changing the organization of professional work, especially in the cultural and creative industries. She has conducted extensive field studies in news organizations in Italy, France, Denmark and Sweden, examining how new technologies shape the ongoing negotiations between journalism and management and how the concept of media independence is translated into practice.

Signe Jernberg is Senior Lecturer in business administration at the University of Gävle. Her research focuses on the organization and governance of universities and other organizations in the Swedish public sector. Signe has led a number of research projects on processes through which universities and colleges gain their status as autonomous actors. She has a particular interest in university administration and collegiality as a form of governance.

Charlotta Kronblad is Postdoctoral Researcher at the Department of Applied Information Technology at the University of Gothenburg and the House of Innovation at the Stockholm School of Economics. She received her PhD from Chalmers University of Technology in Gothenburg. Her thesis focused on the digital transformation of the legal field and examined the consequences of digitalization for business models, working methods and society at large. Her current research lies at the intersection of law, management and digital technology, and her research projects are aimed at both the private and public sectors.

Acknowledgements

This book is the result of a research project financed by Afa Insurance. The project was conducted primarily at the Department of Business Studies, Uppsala University, and at the Gothenburg Research Institute and the Academy of Art and Design, both at the University of Gothenburg. Researchers and colleagues from other universities, such as the University of Gävle and the Stockholm School of Economics, also participated in and contributed to the production of this book. We would like to thank Signe Jernberg and Charlotta Kronblad, who have each contributed an in-depth chapter to the book. Their texts on how staff at Swedish libraries and Swedish courts adapted their work during the pandemic not only complement our own material but also offer the opportunity to step into two areas that have stood out in terms of maintaining the democratic structures and principles on which our society is based. Special appreciation goes also to Gustav Hansson, our former master's student from Uppsala University, who helped us gather and analyse newspaper articles and other secondary data on the pandemic in Sweden.

Colleagues at our respective universities and participants in seminars, workshops and conferences where we have presented parts of the book in different formats also deserve a big thank you for their insights and suggestions on how we could improve it. Seminar discussions about our texts have been an important step in interpreting the results and developing the reasoning around them. Our thanks also go to Ellinor Skagegård, who patiently proofread our manuscript, and to Julia Cechal, Linda Rosenqvist and Mattias Gallagher for their transcription skills.

However, the biggest thank you goes to all those who participated in our study. It cannot have been easy to share their thoughts, experiences, feelings and reflections on perhaps the most tumultuous time in their lives. But without the time, commitment and goodwill that we encountered along the way from some 75 women and men from different parts of the Swedish public welfare sector, this project could not have been realized, and this book could not have been written. Whether we met you via Zoom, by phone, at your workplaces, in your homes, on dog walks or through your recordings and diary entries, we thank you all very much. This book is mainly for you!

Preface

As this book was being written in the spring of 2023, the pandemic and its effects on people's health, labour, economy and general well-being seemed increasingly distant. Russia's attack on Ukraine and the subsequent humanitarian, political and economic consequences for both Ukraine and large parts of Europe have gradually come to overshadow and minimize both the daily and longer-term challenges posed by COVID-19. At the same time, the historic heatwaves of recent years and the growing energy crisis have been reminders that pandemics represent just one of the many serious and existential risks facing humanity – not least as a result of the unsustainable use and overexploitation of our planet. In this way, COVID-19 remains an illustration of the vulnerability and exposure built into our way of life, where risks cannot be isolated within or confined to individual groups, sectors or places. The pandemic and other global crises – both geographical and cultural – thus challenge the conditions for and relations between different parts of the world and society. Various attempts to contain crises and mitigate their effects have, in many respects, pitted cities against rural areas, private activities against public ones and economic interests against democratic, ecological and/or cultural values.

Global crises also risk challenging trust in key institutions like government, universities and the media, as well as the national and international structures and partnerships within which these institutions are embedded (Borraz and Jacobsson, 2023; Hole and Bakken, 2022; Lindblad, Lindqvist, Runesdotter and Wärvik, 2021). Examples include difficulties in agreeing at the EU level on common measures to prevent the spread of the virus or to coordinate the development, production and distribution of COVID-19 vaccines; the breakdown of negotiations on the distribution of migrants from Syria in 2016; and the so far meagre results of efforts to deliver on the Paris Agreement (an international treaty for addressing climate change, signed in 2015 by member states in the United Nations) at local and global levels. These are just a few examples of crisis-related failures that have occurred while trust in these institutions has dropped to historically low levels.

We hope our book, which describes how individuals responsible for large parts of our welfare system on a daily basis dealt with the COVID-19 pandemic, further contributes to the discussions on crises in the public sector that have dominated public debate in recent years. As such, the book aligns with both the Swedish Corona Commission's final report and numerous research studies that state our collective crisis preparedness leaves much to be desired.

However, during the collection of material for this book, another image has become more prominent: that of a Sweden where the ability to face and manage unforeseen crises is largely in the hands of people who, within the framework of their professions and occupations, care for our schools, health centres and hospitals, universities, libraries, retirement homes, family and youth centres and refugee centres, among other publicly funded activities. The stories and narratives on which the book is based testify to individuals who – despite a lack of support and protective equipment, scarce and contradictory information and procedures ill-adapted to the crisis – offered their commitment, their knowledge, their professional skills and, not least, their bodies to help us through the pandemic.

Working on this book has been both a labour of love and a privilege. On one hand, we have been able to work at a relatively safe distance from the workplaces and environments that have been hardest hit, thus not having to endanger our well-being to stop the spread of the virus or cope with its effects. On the other hand, we have been able to rely daily on the public sector in Sweden – as well as in Italy, Poland and the Czech Republic – to care for us, our families, our friends and our colleagues. But we have also experienced severe losses when the efforts of health professionals, teachers, counsellors and aid workers were not enough, and when the public sector exposed weaknesses that were previously hidden or ignored. For us, as social scientists, writing in a detached and neutral way has been a challenging ambition from the outset. How could we say anything about the world we are trying to understand if not through commitment, curiosity and even proximity to the people we met during the study?

Thus, working on this book has also been an exercise in finding how the interpretations and reflections we have made throughout the stories we have collected could be understood in their specific context and in relation to a broader discussion about the pandemic and its impact on societies. We also hope that being part of the pandemic-affected welfare that we describe and interpret has helped us to convey a sense of urgency, humility and gratitude to those who participated in the study with their stories.

We hope that our interpretations contribute to a more nuanced picture of public work during the pandemic and, above all, how welfare sector employees adapted, adjusted their methods and sometimes even defied challenges in their everyday work to continue delivering welfare services. Just as the country's nurses and teachers, who often spoke out in media reports, on their own blogs or in scientific reports, as well as the librarians, IT managers, municipal managers, environmental inspectors, family counsellors and others we met in our study, have also gone a long way in ascribing hero status – or as it is often expressed in our material – the pandemic thus helped welfare staff to make visible the often underestimated, underfunded and stressful work they have always done: 'You are obviously making an effort. You have to remind yourself of that. But when you're in it, it's just my job, I think. I find it very strange when people talk about us as "heroes"' (from a conversation with a nurse, August 2020).

Barbara Czarniawska, Josef Pallas and Elena Raviola
Uppsala and Gothenburg
March 2023

1

In the Shadow of the Pandemic

The idea for this book was first articulated on 21 March 2020. The idea arose partly from our own sense of inadequacy: as Swedish citizens, we wanted to do something meaningful in the fight against COVID-19. But as researchers, we also realized there was a unique opportunity to document the pandemic's impact on people working in various parts of society. In particular, we thought about the people who were seen as working in the shadow of the pandemic – in the areas of the welfare state that are not usually associated with professions and occupations fighting COVID-19 'on the front line'. As social scientists who have studied the Swedish public welfare sector for many years, we saw an opportunity to observe how work tasks and working conditions were being challenged and changed while the virus was spreading in society. These challenges and changes not only concerned healthcare professionals but also teachers, librarians, childcare staff, government investigators, municipal administrators and many other professional groups in this sector.

Our feelings and ambitions were not unique. The journalistic and scientific production of articles and news reports from both outside and within the public sector began to emerge almost simultaneously with the first confirmed cases in Sweden. One national newspaper, *Dagens Nyheter*, published a series of reports titled 'Key workers', another, *Svenska Dagbladet*, 'A month in intensive care'; Swedish television broadcast *Stories from the Frontline*, and the evening paper *Expressen* published a series of articles under the heading 'Inside the pandemic'. These texts and features provided close insights into the work and working environment of welfare professionals (especially those working in health and elderly care). They were soon joined by other newspapers and magazines which quickly adapted their editorial work to cover the pandemic and its progress through public and private Sweden (Ghersetti and Odén, 2021).

Alongside journalistic efforts, COVID-related stories began to take the form of books and reports from within the welfare sector itself. In 2021, the think tank Arena Idé published a report entitled 'On the front line of the coronavirus crisis' which focused on the hard-pressed and under-equipped working conditions of healthcare staff. The same year also saw the publication of Fredrik Sandin Carlson's photo book *På liv och död: berättelser från en pandemi* (Life and death: stories from a pandemic), which provides a poignant image of how members of Kommunal – the public sector's trade union – were dealing with the pandemic in various welfare areas such as healthcare, elderly care and schools. Similarly, staff at the first care home in the southern county of Scania to be seriously affected by COVID-19 shared their experiences in the book *Dansa med corona: om 47 intensiva dagar på vård- och omsorgsboendet Östergård 2* (Dancing with corona: 47 intensive days in the care home at Östergård 2).

These articles, reports and books emphasized how strenuous and exhausting working conditions were for care workers, teachers, gravediggers and cleaners, among many other public sector workers. They also stressed the importance of the work that people in various welfare professions and occupations do for patients, passengers, parents and relatives: all that 'work we have taken for granted', to quote the former president of Kommunal, Tobias Baudin.[1]

Our academic colleagues also quickly produced and disseminated knowledge about the new virus and its impact on the public sector and those working in publicly funded welfare organizations. A Google Scholar search for 'Sweden, COVID-19, public sector, working conditions and professions' in 2020 produced over 100 scientific articles and reports and close to 1,000 in the next two years.[2] Given the slow review and publication processes in academia, these figures alone show just how intensive work efforts were, as well as the extent of the research interest in the pandemic's consequences for the Swedish public sector. Yet a review of these studies showed that this interest was somewhat limited in its focus and scope. Although there were some studies of working conditions in publicly funded activities such as transport, culture, libraries and the court system, the focus was primarily on healthcare, elderly care and schools. Most studies were also geographically limited to the metropolitan regions.

It is easy to understand why much of the research published during this period was relatively brief and episodic in nature. More in-depth studies of the pandemic's long-term effects and how it affected public sector professions and occupations can only be produced now the pandemic has ended. But regardless of the scope and quality of the studies carried out, they showed clearly that there were no areas where the pandemic had not changed the working lives of everyone whose work ensures that the Swedish welfare system continues to deliver services to ten and a half million people every day. The most notable changes were, of course, those related to the digitalization of everything from doctors' appointments to food inspections, and to the enforced transition to remote work.

In the next chapter, we return to the lessons from this early research in more detail. But we can already conclude that the pandemic has changed the form and content of the work of the welfare professions – if not fundamentally, then certainly in a profound way. The pandemic has also redefined the boundaries between what is defined as private and working life; it challenged the view of what constitutes the basis of many professions' core tasks and main responsibilities, and it affected welfare professionals' opportunities to design their physical and virtual workplaces, work processes, routines and even relationships with their colleagues, managers and other professions.

Against this background, one might ask what three organization scholars can contribute to a still ongoing, rich and intense public and academic debate. We hope that our contribution is closely related to our speciality: we study how public sector organizations, and the various professional groups working there, are governed and managed and how they plan, organize and carry out their activities. To approach how people in the Swedish welfare sector have dealt with the impact of the pandemic on their work and their workplaces, we formulated the following goals:

- to pay attention to the work of the professionals who worked 'behind the scenes' (not 'on the front line') of the pandemic;
- to pay attention to the work of these professionals in both large and small municipalities;
- to observe if, and in such cases how, the work of these professionals has changed over the course of the pandemic;
- to establish whether people in various occupational groups have been able to influence their organizations and their working environments to help them deal with the pandemic;
- to reflect on the potential effects of all these experiences on the management of future crises.

A book is born – about our study, our field material and our way of writing

On 23 March 2020, amid the first wave of the pandemic, we sent out a request – via social media, on our respective university websites and through personal contacts – to various authorities, municipalities and state-owned companies asking if anybody was interested in participating in our study. We explained that we were looking for material that would help us understand how the working life of public sector employees had changed during the first period of COVID-19. The response was more meagre than we expected. We had probably underestimated the time and, above all, the energy it takes to reflect daily on one's own work situation and to document these thoughts. Nevertheless, we received quite a few observations in the form of written reflections, activity accounts, diary entries, pictures, poem-like texts and even links to Facebook and Instagram entries where nurses, teachers, care assistants, artists and others documented their 'corona days'. As this type of material continued to appear in our inboxes, we decided to supplement it with more structured interviews.

We conducted our first interviews in early June 2020 and continued interviewing during the summer and autumn of that year. The focus of these interviews was on the relationship between changes in the organization, management and implementation of work tasks and the increased – or decreased – scope of responsibility and autonomy bestowed on professional groups during the initial months of the pandemic (Dimond, 2021). Our questions were primarily designed to help us understand the challenges our interviewees faced in their work during the first months of the pandemic, if and how they confronted these challenges and what support they received from their colleagues, managers and regional and state authorities. We also asked how our interviewees chose which aspects of their work to prioritize; how did they feel, and how did they manage their emotions? These interviews, together with the self-reported narratives, account for about half of the material. In total, between March and October 2020 we collected 35 testimonies from persons working in municipalities – in particular municipal welfare services – state-owned companies, regional councils, central authorities and political parties.

After analysing this material (which we reported on in our chapter 'Pandemicracy and organizing in unsettling times'[3]), we realized that the pandemic not only posed challenges to various parts of the public sector and to various professions and occupations but that there were also geographical variations in how these challenges were perceived and managed. We have summarized our reflections as follows:

- There was a wide variation of changes in the working lives of different occupations and professions. This variation seemed to depend partly on professional and geographical distance from the pandemic.
- Some public sector organizations focused on their core mission and activities (at least at the beginning of the pandemic), while others increased the number and kind of their procedures and control measures (usually in compliance with pandemic-related measures).
- Professional expertise was central to many COVID-19-related actions, but it was also combined with commitment, emotional involvement and 'activism', which sometimes challenged traditional professional-administrative structures and practices.
- The everyday work of public servants was seriously affected by the international and national media attention and the disseminated images of Sweden and its pandemic strategy.

- Professional work was the main factor in the relatively high resilience to the effects of the pandemic, thanks to which public sector organizations were largely able to continue their activities, albeit in modified forms.
- There was also a 'bouncing back effect': when the reaction to the crisis had stabilized, there was a strong desire to return to the pre-crisis state among both managers and practitioners.

Thus, we decided that in our further work we would focus on differences between various occupational groups and between geographical areas. At the end of October 2020, we applied for a grant from the think tank Ada Försäkring. In the application, we explained that our main purpose was to study how various occupational groups and professions that were operating 'behind the front line' (the pandemic), and in more peripheral localities, managed their work. We intended to include three types of professions and occupations:

- Occupations and professions that were directly exposed to the effects of the pandemic, such as those in healthcare. These would serve as a reference point to better understand the work of professionals and other employees working under different circumstances and conditions.
- Occupations and professions that were indirectly affected by the pandemic, but where these secondary effects were still significant (for example, teachers, childcare staff, social workers, military and emergency services staff).
- Occupations and professions working with issues relatively distant from the areas affected by the pandemic, but which had been reorganized in the shadow of the pandemic (for example, social services administrators, family counsellors, counsellors, librarians and publicly funded culture workers).

We selected interviewees among professionals from both large and small municipalities. We also attempted to cover most of the country, as the geographical location was clearly one of the aspects that affected the working conditions of certain professions and occupations and the ability of their members to devote themselves to the tasks and assignments they were responsible for.

In our grant application, we also argued that many professions and occupations in our public sector have in recent decades been affected by major political reforms, resulting in increased demands for efficiency, reporting and thus tighter control, as well as a zeal for evaluation (Blomgren and Waks, 2017). At the same time, public sector organizations were subject to an influx of various governance and management ideas from the private sector. These reforms had positive and negative effects for both users and staff, but they have undoubtedly limited the autonomy of welfare staff and thus their ability to exercise their professional expertise (Jansson and Parding, 2011).

Referring to our analysis of the field material from 2020, we therefore raised the question of whether pandemic-related measures undertaken in the public sector were related to working methods and forms of governance that have become popular in the aftermath of what is usually called New Public Management. Thus, our project might also be relevant for political discussions about how the Swedish public sector should be governed to strengthen its resilience to future risks and threats.

Zooming, travelling and observing remotely

In December 2020, we were informed that our application had been approved, and we started the second phase of the project. We began by contacting municipalities that might be interested in participating in the project. These were municipalities that met our requirements in terms of size and geographical spread, and where the municipal leaders would help us contact employees in various municipal welfare organizations. As we were still in a pandemic and had a long way to go before large parts of the population received their first dose of vaccine, we used Zoom as our main tool. When the vaccination programme started on a larger scale in the spring of 2021, we were able to go out and hold some interviews face-to-face, albeit to a limited extent. Still, between April 2021 and June 2022 we had the opportunity to conduct interviews and visit five municipalities.

During this period, we conducted 40 interviews with people working in different areas of municipal welfare and visited each of the five municipalities at least once. Such two- to three-day visits were intended to give us a better understanding of the various workplaces described in the interviews. Before each visit, we read newspaper articles in the local press, official statistics, websites, reports and other documents to give us a picture of the issues and challenges that each municipality had faced.

As the welfare activities in the municipalities visited were generally spread over a large geographical area, and as the time was not yet ripe for travelling on public transport, our main mode of transport was the car. As well as giving us the opportunity to visit workplaces that were far away from the town centre, we were also allowed, on several occasions, to visit people in their home offices, to accompany them on assignments such as environmental inspections and to witness the difficulties of crossing the then closed border between Sweden and Norway. During our stays, we were also able to visit the often empty municipal libraries, browse municipal information material while sitting in the receptions of the municipal administrations and enter health centres and care homes wearing face masks. We were also allowed to sit in classrooms furnished with protective measures against COVID-19 and observe local council meetings. We took walks past municipal childcare centres, schools, leisure centres and other facilities that had some outdoor activities. One of us took a dog on such walks, which often led to spontaneous conversations with the personnel at these organizations, making the meetings feel more natural.

Writing a story about working in the shadow of the pandemic

Combined with the first interviews, our material includes 57 interviews from nine municipalities, 11 interviews from seven state authorities and seven interviews with staff in regional and state organizations.

The interviews in municipalities were conducted with officials who held various administrative functions, such as case officers, unit and IT managers and committee secretaries, and within a wide range of public organizations, such as schools, social services, libraries, local authorities and primary care centres. The municipalities included in the project differed in size from very small (a few thousand inhabitants) to some of the largest in the country. They are geographically dispersed across Sweden from north to south and from west to east and have been affected by COVID-19 at different times and with different consequences for their population, economy, culture and governance.

Among the 11 government officials we interviewed, some worked in the armed forces, others in the higher education sector and still others in the migration authority. At regional and state level, we spoke mainly to healthcare professionals, as well as to employees from a state-owned company, a museum and the Swedish Parliament. Overall, our material includes interviews with people from the following occupations and professions:

- asylum officers
- building inspectors
- business developers
- chairpersons of municipal boards
- council and municipal secretaries
- doctors
- educators
- employment officers
- environmental and health protection inspectors
- environmental managers
- family counsellors
- head teachers
- heads of units for child and youth services
- information advisors

- IT managers
- librarians
- municipal directors
- nurses
- personnel managers
- politicians
- public health coordinators
- researchers
- social coordinators
- social secretaries
- social services managers
- teachers
- technical administrators
- university lecturers
- youth workers

We also invited two of our colleagues who study libraries and courtrooms to add their reflections on the changes provoked by COVID-19. The reason we chose to include these two chapters is that they explicitly confirm what we have found in our own material, but in much more detail. What we wanted to illustrate was that the pandemic also impacted work in the Swedish public sector in terms of society's core democratic processes, principles and values. We realized that certain aspects of Swedish democracy were challenged, and in some respects even limited, when municipal administrations, schools and libraries adapted their activities to the progress of the pandemic, and that this democratic deficit deserved special attention. Our colleagues' methods are specified in the Appendices.

All field material presented in this book has been anonymized to protect the personal integrity of those who have chosen to share their stories and to assure them that they cannot be identified. Although we informed our interlocutors both in speech and in writing of the purpose and design of the project, stressing that our aim was not to evaluate either them or their organizations, it was at times noticeable that they wondered how open they could be. We assured them that all material would be anonymized, that original recordings would be deleted after transcription and that they could withdraw their participation at any time during the study. When processing our material, we have therefore tried, as far as possible, to remove all information that could be used to identify individuals, workplaces and organizations.

The structure of the book

As we explained in the Preface, this book is intended to serve as a contemporary document showing how the pandemic has come to affect the working lives of hundreds of thousands of public sector employees. We hope that, even when it acquires a historical character, it will be of interest to scholars studying how public sectors function in times of crises and threats.

In the next chapter, we place our study in a broader context of general studies of the pandemic, to which we return in the two concluding chapters. The main part of the book contains an interpreted documentation of how welfare work was organized during the pandemic in which we weave together a chronological structure with thematic presentations, identifying some central themes of 'pandemic work'. Chapters 3–6 describe in chronological order the work of civil servants during the pandemic as a journey from 'the extraordinary' to 'the new normal'. Chapter 7 focuses on the role of digitalization of work, as this was a key metamorphosis that state and municipal organizations and their staff underwent during the pandemic. In Chapter 8, we describe how pandemic-related problems and solutions were handled in our schools. Chapter 9, authored by Signe Jernberg, describes the peculiarities of Swedish libraries, showing their important democratic mission that was first challenged and then managed during the pandemic. In Chapter 10, Charlotta Kronblad shows what happens when institutional forms for the exercise of justice must move to digital courtrooms.

In the book's penultimate chapter (11), we apply an organizational and governance perspective to analyse changes in the relationship between state and regional authorities and municipalities on the one hand and public sector staff on the other, under the extraordinary conditions created by the pandemic. The last chapter (12) presents our idea of 'pandemicracy' in the hope that it will become a starting point for further discussions about the necessity for new forms of governance and organization in the public sector. The concept of pandemicracy attempts to cover both the ways in which the pandemic has affected the formal organization and governance of the welfare sector (bureaucracy) and the ways in which the public sector fulfils its societal mission (democracy). In the Epilogue, we suggest how experiences from the pandemic can be used in a discussion on what future welfare could, should and is likely to be.

2

The Public Sector and the Pandemic: The State of Knowledge

The stories collected in our project are rooted in the unique path that Sweden took to deal with the COVID-19 pandemic. There are divergent views on how the 'Swedish strategy' – and its impact on society – differs from how other countries acted – not least in terms of recommendations, restrictions and the relatively voluntary use of protective measures such as distancing, face masks and hygiene procedures (Anderberg, 2021). Nevertheless, it is the case that there were distinctive aspects to the Swedish strategy that gave rise to political, public and academic debate and constitute a background against which the pandemic work of the welfare professions and professions should be understood (Aucante, 2022). The management of the pandemic was linked to a number of principles that allocate responsibilities and roles to different parts of the Swedish public administration. These principles were originally intended to lead to some variation when put into practice (Borraz and Jacobsson, 2023).

The primary principle is that the government relies on the expertise of the country's expert authorities when formulating its policies and that regions and municipalities have considerable autonomy when interpreting these policies. This applies even in times of crisis (Jacobsson, 2020; SOU, 2022: 10a). What this means in practice becomes easier to understand if we relate Sweden's crisis management to how the Swedish administrative model works in general. Public administration is shaped and carried out by municipalities, regions and the state. The regions are primarily responsible for healthcare, which also includes the prevention and control of diseases. Municipalities are legally responsible for certain aspects of primary care, elderly care, education, social services, infrastructure, rescue services, emergency preparedness and civil defence, environmental and health protection and other matters (Local Government Act 2017:725). The state administration has a regulatory, scrutinizing and evaluating role. As a result, large parts of the country's public sector are designed according to laws, regulations and recommendations that are based on the knowledge provided to the government by the responsible expert authorities (Cameron and Jonsson-Cornell, 2020).

These frameworks, regulations and recommendations – to the extent that they are not strictly binding – are then interpreted by regions and municipalities based on various local and regional conditions, such as the prevailing political situation, economy, geography and demography. Such autonomy and relative freedom vis-à-vis the central government administration are particularly extensive in welfare areas that fall under municipal self-government and which, in addition to services such as schools, elderly care and healthcare, also include physical planning, public transport, housing provision and business development (Regeringsformen, 1974: 152; SKR, 2021a, 2021b).

By extension, this governance model and its related central focus on the principle of responsibility and proximity – that is, decisions concerning public affairs should be made by and in relation to those most affected and responsible – imply that even in times of crisis, regions and municipalities are (for the most part) responsible for designing their strategies and approaches to meet the challenges and problems that arise during, or in connection with, crisis. This model also implies that the responsibility for planning and implementing the welfare commitments of regions and municipalities should rest largely on the expertise, proven knowledge and professional skills of those closest to the affected areas. The relatively independent role that government agencies, regions and municipalities have in relation to ministries and the government is largely based on using the knowledge and experience of welfare professionals in shaping the form and content of the welfare work that authorities, regions and municipalities provide for their citizens.

How the public sector is intended to function – both in normal times and in times of crisis – places a significant responsibility on professions and professional groups within this sector. However, in recent decades, Sweden has pushed for reforms that, in many respects, have worsened the conditions in which this responsibility can be maintained and developed (Greve et al, 2020; Kuhlmann et al, 2021). Teachers, nurses, doctors, social workers, administrators, researchers and the other occupations and professions we usually associate with the public welfare sector have long been affected by increased administrative burdens and practices, paperwork and demands for constant adaptation to new management tools and strategies (Forssell and Ivarsson Westenberg, 2014; Bornemark, 2018).

Through formal requirements for increased efficiency, measurements, evaluation and documentation, professions and professionals in the welfare sector have increasingly been given less room to perform their work autonomously and on the basis of their expertise (Ahlbäck Öberg et al, 2016; Jakobsson et al, 2020). These requirements are legitimized and internalized, not least through a continuous influx of ideas and ideologies coming mainly from the private sector, from which public organizations frequently hire and recruit managers, consultants, business developers, economists and other experts and specialists. In the most extreme cases, this influx of management knowledge serves as a tool to actively limit the influence of the welfare professions on how, and on the basis of which values, their work is organized and designed. In a study of Karolinska Hospital, Grafström and her colleagues showed the consequences of this inflow of 'management knowledge' on the quality of care provided and on the overall functioning of the hospital. They found that the medical profession was largely ignored when consultants from Boston Consulting Group were given free rein to design everything from patient flows, care priorities, pricing of procedures and treatments and quality evaluations to recruitment and documentation (Grafström et al, 2021; see also Gustavsson and Röstlund, 2019).

Yet studies of other areas of the public sector have also highlighted how occupational groups and professions such as teachers, police officers, administrators, social services staff and other welfare workers are continuously and systematically questioned on the basis of, and with the help of, the introduction and spread of various management methods and neo-bureaucratic models and practices (Hall, 2012; Bringselius, 2017). The research conducted within the framework of the Trust Delegation (a committee created by the government for the improvement of local government) and other studies of welfare professions (for example, Alvehus and Loodin, 2020; Pallas and Fredriksson, 2020) indicates that modern management-bureaucratic rationalization makes contemporary public organizations and their governance increasingly complex and 'de-professionalized' (Lægreid and Verhoest, 2010). Most of the research findings show that such complexity in public organizations has coincided with – and to a large extent also contributed to – the increasing introduction of new, and the expansion of existing, administrative tasks and routines over the last couple of decades (Forssell and Ivarsson Westerberg, 2014). Instead of strengthening the professional skills and knowledge of key staff, the management of public organizations has focused on increased control, evaluation and coordination of professional work (Agevall and Olofsson, 2020; Greve et al, 2020).

As organizations become more complex, the roles within them often become professionalized. This professionalisation does not simply imply the development of increased knowledge and skills necessary in the provision of public services. It is instead defined as focusing on strengthening the management and administrative functions within organizations where welfare staff work (Ahlbäck Öberg and Bringselius, 2015). This professionalization takes form through centralizing decisions and moving decision making higher up in the organizations, to where professional administrators and staff in increasingly specialized support functions such as IT, human resources, communication and, of course, professional leaders and managers are recruited (Agevall and Olofsson, 2020; Eriksson and Ivarsson-Westerberg, 2021).

Based on this brief overview, it is relatively easy to imagine that, when facing the pandemic, the professions within the Swedish public sector – and in particular those at the core of the Swedish welfare system– did so with 'one hand tied behind their back'. Welfare workers and many welfare professions were largely deprived of control over their work and the organizational context in which it was carried out. In the following chapters, we allow personal narratives to play a more prominent role in describing and discussing how the public sector was able to continue to function even under the special conditions created by the pandemic. In these chapters, we point to the tensions between professional expertise and the organizational constraints that municipal administrators, environmental inspectors, teachers, nurses, family therapists and other welfare professionals had to deal with and overcome.

There are, of course, many more dimensions than those mentioned here that affected how agencies, municipalities and their personnel dealt with the effects of COVID-19. These not only include the limited financial and material resources allocated by the central government, continuous policy and governance reforms, rapid development and implementation of welfare technologies and long-term skills shortages in many welfare sectors (Wolmesjö and Solli, 2021) but also more general societal trends that, in various ways, constitute conditions for the public sector as a whole. Changing public demands and expectations on publicly funded services (Solli et al, 2020) or increased confidence in 'welfare markets', where users and providers are expected to relate to each other on the basis of 'free customer choice', diversity and competition (Meagher and Szebehely, 2019), are just a few examples. However, since we can assume that these aspects of public sector provisionwere less noticeable in the everyday life of the pandemic, we have chosen to leave them out of the framework of the discussion we seek to conduct in this book.

In the remainder of this chapter, we briefly describe what our colleagues who were somewhat faster have been able to write about how the public sector and people within it came to deal with the pandemic. Many of the texts already published confirm what we have seen in the stories we have collected, and the empirical illustrations on which these texts are based provide a background against which our own material can be read and discussed.

Welfare professions in times of crisis

The first publications with a more explicit focus on the non-medical effects of the pandemic appeared as early as 2020. Most of these studies examined, from different perspectives, how the Swedish government organized and coordinated both its own efforts and efforts within and between various ministries, authorities and parts of the publicly financed welfare system (Aucante, 2022). Studies in healthcare, elderly care, education, social services and other welfare areas showed that different, and often contradictory, instructions and directives on how to act when the pandemic became a fact were issued from central sources. As well as the government and its various ministries (Askim and Bergström, 2022) and authorities such as the Public Health Authority, the National Board of Health and Welfare and the Health and Care Inspectorate, criticism of this information and communication deficit has also been directed at employer organizations such as the Swedish Association of Local Authorities and Regions, Almega and Sobona, as well as those individuals who were most directly responsible in the municipalities, also received their fair share of critical remarks.[1] Many employees in the welfare professions experienced a lack of information, insufficient resources and weak support while dealing with the practical challenges and continuing to deliver services to their students, patients, asylum seekers, victims of crime and the users and recipients of other state and municipal social services (Huupponen, 2020; SOU, 2022; Kreitz-Sandberg, Nils and Fredriksson, 2022).

The results from existing studies indicate that uncertainty gradually decreased as new procedures were introduced and old procedures and working methods began to be adapted to the new conditions. This adaptation was particularly visible where the digitalization of the work of welfare professions could be accelerated (for example, in schools and healthcare), which in many respects also changed the conditions for municipalities' efforts in other contexts. In its report on eHealth and welfare technology in municipalities, the National Board of Health and Welfare comments that the pandemic contributed to a faster transition to digital tools. Above all, it was in relation to the ability of municipal staff to carry out parts of their work remotely, increased opportunities for supervision and documentation, as well as skills development and collaboration that the accelerated digitalization came into use (National Board of Health and Welfare, 2021). Another, and perhaps somewhat unexpected, consequence of digitalization seems to be that workplace-related conflicts and vulnerability in the form of bullying, violations and harassment increased and spread (Alvinius and Bengt, 2022).

Virtually all studies that focus on the assurance and implementation of various publicly funded welfare services emphasize changed working conditions as being central to the ability to respond to the pandemic without bringing large parts of the public sector to its knees (Engwall and Storm, 2021). The results of the various studies indicate that the pandemic has had a revealing effect in that it has clearly shown both the shortcomings and the strengths of public sector organizations – not least in relation to the working conditions that constitute the everyday life of many of the welfare professions. Lessons from the pandemic confirm the previously expressed criticism that professional work has come to be limited and bounded by increasingly administration-oriented public sector organizations such as government agencies and municipalities, that is, organizations that have an increasingly prominent role in how public services are to be designed and provided (see also Jernberg and Pallas, 2022).

Under 'normal' conditions, welfare work is characterized by its reliance on formal coordination, policies, rules and administrative procedures. However, during the pandemic, the continuity and stability of public service provision seems to have become more dependent on the professional expertise, commitment and loyalty of public sector employees. Thorgersen and Mars (2021) show how music teachers had to change the form and content of their work when physical conditions (such as school closures) and organizational support (lack of structures for collegial exchange and collaboration) changed dramatically at the beginning of the pandemic. In a study on recruitment in municipal elderly care involving 13 municipalities, Sunna Lundberg (2021) showed that recruitment needs increased during the pandemic, mainly for experienced staff who could handle areas where municipalities and care homes lacked expertise. The lack of staff required many people with lower or less relevant skills and experiences to step in and be trained in areas such as infection prevention and control, respiratory support and anxiety management. Existing staff had to compensate for the inability of municipalities and nursing homes were unable to provide the necessary resources, competencies and skills.

When formal organizational settings and contexts in many government agencies and municipalities became inadequate or even contradictory, hundreds of thousands of public sector employees found themselves handling their responsibilities under conditions that were unlike anything they had experienced before. As expectations and demands for schools, hospitals, health centres, family centres and libraries to ensure the continuity and expansion of their services grew, the responsibility for these services shifted to those working closest to the users – regardless of whether the latter were pupils, patients, theatregoers, asylum seekers or recipients of social support.

The pandemic measures implemented in many public organizations had unprecedented consequences for their employees' working conditions. Many saw their working practices and professional values and preferences not only challenged but also threatened, as the pandemic made it impossible to ensure the necessary support, equipment, instructions or even safe working conditions. Adapting to the pandemic also required employees in government agencies, municipalities, state and municipal companies and other public sector organizations to acquire knowledge and new skills on their own rather than through formal support from their organizations (Erlandsson et al, 2023).

Among the main pandemic-related adaptations were the increased online presence and the use of various digital tools for meetings, collaboration, monitoring, recruitment, training and so on. With these tools, many people's social and working, lives moved to the virtual world, leading to increased needs for investment in technological equipment and digital services, as well as the development and use of new types of knowledge and skills. Finding, downloading and learning how to use new tools and software also increased the time needed to plan and carry out tasks. Technology stress, work overload and the need to be constantly connected also had negative effects on people's physical and mental health (De' et al, 2020).

Data from the first years of the pandemic indicate that the work of many occupational groups and professions intensified in terms of extended workloads and longer working hours (De' et al, 2020). This may seem paradoxical, given the dramatic economic downturn caused by the pandemic both in Sweden and internationally (SOU, 2022: 10). A survey of five government agencies in 2020 (Hiselius and Arnfalk, 2021) showed that government staff often found it relatively easy to start or expand their remote work in order to fulfil their work tasks. For many people, phasing out travel and physical meetings, and at the same time getting used to and developing various digital forms of collaboration, was something that was already 'in the air', as their organizations were already in the process of launching digital and remote forms of working before the pandemic (Carlsson et al, 2021).

But changing working conditions also led public sector workers (like most other workers) to make adjustments outside the scope of their professional and occupational commitments. As the pandemic contributed to the collapse of traditional work–life boundaries, many people found it difficult to find time and space for rest and recovery. The limited ability to separate work-related responsibilities from private life that the pandemic brought to many welfare professions also influenced people's general well-being. Increased intensity, uncertainty, unpredictability, stress, discomfort and even life-threatening working conditions became part of everyday life both within and outside the public sector organizations (Lee, 2021; Fernemark et al, 2022; Tarvis et al, 2022).

Like other front line public services, elderly care personnel did their best to provide care during the pandemic. Practical nurses and care aides did their utmost in unreasonably stressful, precarious and often dangerous conditions (Theobald, 2022: 6).

Welfare professionals' responses to crises

As already mentioned, crises and extraordinary events can expose the challenges that professions and occupations within the public welfare sector have been dealing with in the last couple of decades, but which, under normal circumstances, tend to be ignored or glossed over – often with the help of economic and administrative arguments about the need for lean, efficient and competitive structures and work processes. At the same time, professional skills and knowledge among the staff of government agencies and municipalities seem to be a basic prerequisite for these organizations to be able to continue with their activities and missions in times of uncertainty, turbulence and distress. In his study of public organizations' crisis management, Ödlund (2010) shows that the foundations for being able to cooperate and coordinate work within and between public sector organizations are strongly based on the ability of professions to overcome structural, bureaucratic and cultural differences that arise within and between these organizations due to their specificity, mission and mandate.

Similarly, Weick and Sutcliffe (2011) also observed that it is professional knowledge, and the creation of meaning from that knowledge, that shapes the terms and conditions under which organizations deal with extraordinary events such as disasters, accidents and serious or unexpected disruptions to regular operations. In their book *Managing the Unexpected*, Weick and Sutcliffe show that work in emergency rooms, air traffic control centres and firefighting is highly dependent on building what they call 'reliable organizations' (in today's terminology, we would say 'resilient organizations'). Organizational resilience is, in their view, based on the professional knowledge and skills of doctors, air traffic controllers and firefighters, rather than on formal structures, procedures and leadership.

The importance of interaction and trust between competent professionals and the management of the organizations in which they operate is also evident in studies on the Swedish public sector during the first months of the COVID-19 pandemic. In his study of elderly care in Swedish municipalities, Lundberg (2021) showed that the ability to recruit and retain knowledgeable, experienced and committed staff was the key to successfully managing the (often unexpected) effects of the pandemic. Similar reasoning was also put forward by the Corona Commission in its second interim report (SOU, 2021: 89), which highlighted both the individual and collective efforts that welfare professions have contributed to – not only in applying their formal knowledge but also through their commitment and newly acquired expertise and their ability to deal with problems for which authorities, municipalities and other public actors were not prepared.

Broström and Löfström (2022) investigated five municipalities during the period 2020–21. They found that the most successful ways in which municipalities and their staff were able to deal with pandemic-related challenges were largely linked to a low degree of dependence on planning and formal coordination from regional authorities and central government. Eva Martinsson and colleagues obtained similar results in a study of school nurses, which showed that during the pandemic, collaboration with other professionals in the schools – mainly technical support staff in student health and teachers – was more important and effective than relying on formal municipal and national plans, policies and regulations (Martinsson et al, 2021).

In an investigation of Sweden's handling of three parallel societal crises (climate, migration and COVID-19), Elander and colleagues (2021) highlighted various vulnerabilities associated with these crises. In the report, the authors argue that it is precisely the complexity of the governance relationships between actors at local, regional and central levels that contributes to the difficulty of securing democratically and scientifically based, long-term public interest in welfare-related contexts. Their argument is based on the observation that unique problems arise within the framework of each individual crisis that require professionals at the local level – for example, in municipalities or local authorities – who, by virtue of their expertise and knowledge, are able to bridge the complex governance relationships that these problems often challenge.

These studies strengthen the argument that trust in professional knowledge was not only relevant but a necessary condition for welfare organizations, municipalities and government agencies to handle both the specific and general challenges and problems that emerged during the pandemic. In many areas, this knowledge has also come to challenge and redefine the overall role of formal organizational structures, rules and policies in the organization and governance of public welfare activities.

The purpose of our brief review is not to argue that the professional knowledge, experience and commitment that many welfare professions demonstrated during the pandemic was the only reason the Swedish public sector could continue to function (and in many aspects also evolve) during the pandemic. As has been discussed in numerous academic papers, public inquiries and popular science reports and books published in recent years, explanations for pandemic-related successes and failures in the public sector can be related to many different factors – some to the characteristics of the 'Swedish model', others to its inadequacy. However, whatever the approach, perspective or explanatory model for the question of successful pandemic management, it is difficult not to return to the importance that hundreds of thousands of people have had and continue to have in their capacity as welfare professionals.

3

Waking Up to a New World

'New coronavirus discovered in China'. This was the title of the press release from the Public Health Agency of Sweden on 16 January 2020, at which time it assessed the risk of the infection spreading to Sweden as very low (Public Health Agency, 2020a). The agency pointed out that 'there is not yet reliable evidence of human-to-human transmission', which is required to cause major outbreaks. 'This does not appear to be the case', Anders Tegnell, the state epidemiologist, said in the same press release; he later explained that 'in Sweden, most infection control measures are taken without coercion'. The experience here is that someone who is well-informed and motivated understands and follows the given recommendations and that taking responsibility is better than coercive measures.[1] To remind the reader of the situation at the beginning of 2020, we start the chapter with the first general mentions of the virus, which appeared in the Swedish debate in connection with the World Health Organization's (WHO) declaration on 11 March that COVID-19 was a pandemic.

Chinese origin and safe Sweden

The first general information – from both the authorities and the media – focused on the origin and spread of the virus in the Chinese city of Wuhan. As with previous coronavirus outbreaks, Chinese animal markets, with their unique mix of animals and humans, were identified as a likely cause of the virus's mutation. On 30 January, just days after the WHO classified the COVID-19 outbreak as an international threat to human health, the Public Health Agency of Sweden submitted a formal request to classify the virus as a public and societal danger. However, Anders Carlsson, the Director-General until October 2021, explained that '[t]he classification does not mean that we look at the situation in a more serious way than before. But we want to be able to have all the necessary instruments for dealing with serious diseases.'[2]

But even before the situation in Sweden was seen as serious, and before general recommendations on social distancing were formulated, tourists and other travellers from and to China became a sensitive and controversial issue. There was a strong belief that a ban on entry from China would be sufficient to prevent the spread of infection. The Ministry of Foreign Affairs advised against non-essential travel to Hubei Province in China as early as 26 January 2020, and on 31 January 2020, Scandinavian Airlines stopped all flights to and from Shanghai and Beijing, although travel to and from Hong Kong continued.[3]

Among the general public, however, the threat of the new virus was still abstract and something that was happening on the other side of the world, not here, not now. One person who took the virus more seriously, however, was an environmental inspector in western Sweden, who began discussing the possible spread of the virus to Sweden with his colleagues:

> In early February, I raised the issue of the coronavirus spontaneously with some colleagues, on two occasions. I said that it might be useful to prepare and find out what we needed to do if and when this virus came to us. The interest was non-existent. As I recall, there was also scant information from government authorities at the time. The threat remained abstract and distant. When the infection flared up in the Italian Alps, a popular skiing destination during the winter half-term break, the threat of infection in Sweden started to come closer. (B2, environmental inspector, West)

In January and February 2020, media coverage of the virus largely focused on the number of cases and deaths in China and on whether or not Sweden could be considered at risk. The media – in the spirit of local newspapers – reinforced the idea that the infection was far away and that Swedes had nothing to worry about. Here is the response to a journalist from *Kungälvs-Posten* who asked the chief physician at Kungälv Hospital, Jacob Wulfsberg, if local residents should be worried about the virus: "'No, as things stand now, there is no reason. However, we have a routine to be prepared if cases arise", says Jacob Wulfsberg. "The hospital has protective equipment, an infection room and the staff are updated on the procedures that apply if the infection should reach Kungälv Hospital"' (Lyrstrand Larssen, 2020: 6).

Even when it was reported that the neighbouring village of Ytterby had a suspected case of COVID-19, the response of both the doctors interviewed in the media and the official communication from the Public Health Agency was that this was not something to worry about: 'Sweden is well prepared.' Swedish crisis preparedness was also a hot topic of conversation among public servants in different parts of the welfare sector:

> Previous crises that municipalities and other elements of the public sector had experienced led them to feel prepared for the potential

> future crisis. The 2015 refugee crisis and the forest fires in 2018 were mentioned in some municipalities as examples of crises that had contributed to a good level of preparedness: 'I think it helped a lot in that you know that you have to act even though you don't know everything.' (D14, principal, South East)

Some municipalities had already been working strategically with local crisis response groups, while others started hiring staff with experience of crises, including professional soldiers or expatriates from organizations such as the Red Cross and Médecins Sans Frontières. At North Central, we heard how the municipality succeeded in recruiting a communications director who had previously worked for an aid organization in Africa:

> After the fires [2018] we learnt that crisis communication was key. We looked for someone who had the experience we needed. And XX was perfect. She had many years of experience from being out there and dealing with things that we are not used to ... And she is not the only one, when I think about it. We have someone else here who comes from an aid organization where he worked with refugees. That [hiring staff with experience of crises] might be something to consider more systematically for the future. (D20, deputy director of administration, North Central)

Other municipalities also invested in developing their crisis preparedness by increasing general knowledge about crises and formally training their management teams. One municipal manager in western Sweden told us:

> Even before corona, we worked a lot with crisis preparedness. We have had managerial training and political training on crisis preparedness systems and the demands on the municipality ... We have run certain variants, plus we started to prepare ... There was a major total defence exercise here last year, so we started with the first steps, in autumn 2019. This had been run throughout Sweden, so that society had prepared itself a little bit in any case. (C19, municipal manager, West)

From the perspective of the authorities and municipalities, crisis preparedness meant organizations using the bureaucratic tools available in the Swedish system and having an informed public. The Public Health Agency announced on 31 January 2020 that the classification of the COVID-19 infection as a public and societal danger would be seen as such a tool: it was about putting legislation in place in case the infection started to spread in society.

An informed public was a key pillar of the Swedish preparedness for a crisis. In a reassuring message to the public on 13 February 2020, Anders

Wallensten, epidemiologist at the Public Health Agency, confirmed that 'you don't have to worry about getting infected in Sweden, as we have no spread in the country', and that Sweden had a robust system in place to quickly detect infectious diseases. According to Wallensten, all the public had to do at the time was to keep up to date with the situation in Sweden and other countries through the websites of the Public Health Agency and the Ministry of Foreign Affairs. As the then Minister for Social Affairs, Lena Hallengren, later said at a press conference: 'Correct and factual information. That is society's best weapon.'[4]

However, the authorities and the government were not the only sources of information for the Swedish public (Einhorn, 2022). The media made significant efforts to inform about and debate COVID-19 as the pandemic spread (Figure 3.1).

Figure 3.1 compares the number of articles on the COVID-19 pandemic published in 2020 with the number of intensive care (IC) patients treated in the same year. It shows that despite a similar trend in both measurements, the pandemic remained newsworthy even when the number of IC patients dropped significantly during the summer.

Public sector communication also emphasized that voluntariness is the cornerstone of Swedish infection control work. This is because experience has shown that voluntariness is more successful than coercion, which carries a risk of 'creating fear of seeking care'.[5] 'But since the new coronavirus has been classified as a socially dangerous disease, there are now legal possibilities to use more powerful measures if necessary', Wallensten added.

The crisis is here: the first recommendations and the hunt for equipment

On 11 March 2020, the WHO's Director-General declared in a press release that the extent of the spread of the disease meant it could now be considered a pandemic:

> In the past two weeks, the number of cases of COVID-19 outside China has increased 13-fold, and the number of affected countries has tripled. There are now more than 118,000 cases in 114 countries and 4,291 people have lost their lives. Thousands more are fighting for their lives in hospitals. In the days and weeks ahead, we expect to see the number of cases, the number of deaths, and the number of affected countries climb even higher. WHO has been assessing this outbreak around the clock and we are deeply concerned both by the alarming levels of spread and severity, and by the alarming levels of inaction. We have therefore made the assessment that COVID-19 can be characterised as a pandemic. Pandemic is not a word to use lightly

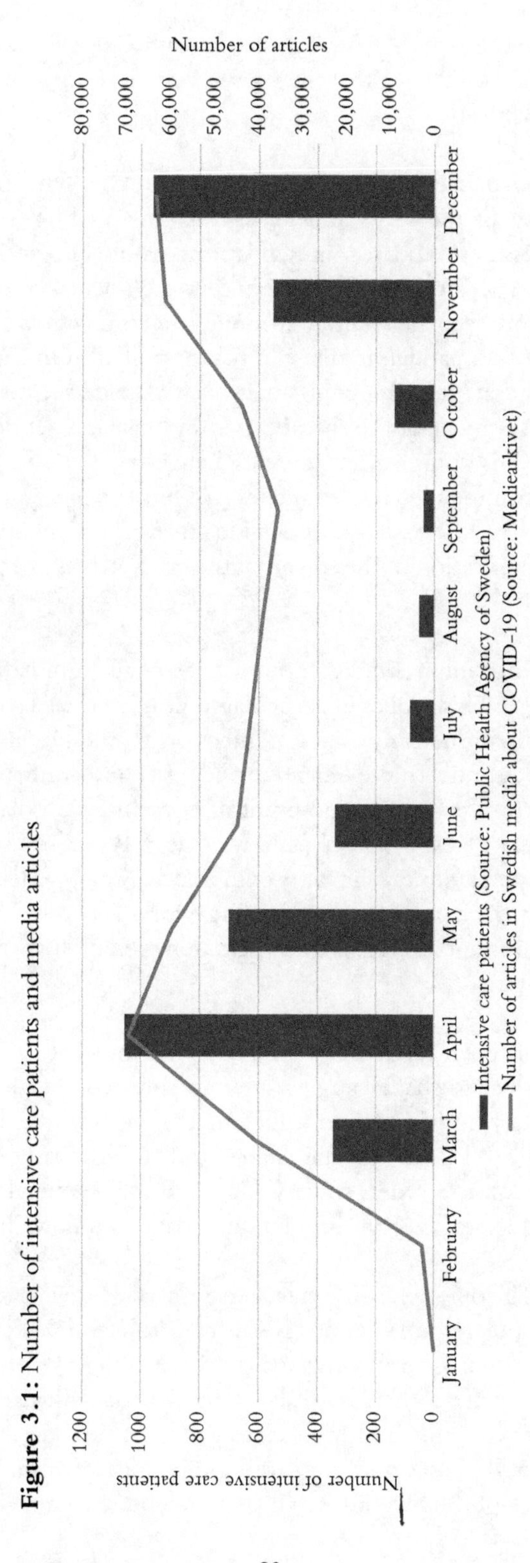

Figure 3.1: Number of intensive care patients and media articles

> or carelessly. It is a word that, if misused, can cause unreasonable fear, or unjustified acceptance that the fight is over, leading to unnecessary suffering and death.[6]

In his speech to the media, he vacillated between pointing to the unpredictability of the virus and reassuring the world that the WHO's upcoming assessment and recommendations would provide a solid basis for countries to act on. On the one hand, the Director-General said, 'we have never before seen a pandemic sparked by a coronavirus', and 'we have never before seen a pandemic that can be controlled'. On the other hand, he emphasized that 'describing the situation as a pandemic does not change the WHO's assessment of the threat posed by this virus. It doesn't change what the WHO is doing, and it doesn't change what countries should do.' The WHO recommended that countries take 'urgent and aggressive action'.

On the same day, the Swedish Public Health Agency issued a press release on the new classification of the spread of the coronavirus as a pandemic but called for calm:

> The WHO has emphasized the importance of all countries preparing for the disease. This applies in particular to healthcare. It also points out that countries in the early stages of infection should not take extreme measures. 'It is much more efficient to identify and confirm cases and trace their contacts, there is no point in governments isolating entire communities or closing schools,' said Michael J. Ryan, head of WHO's emergency preparedness at a press conference. 'For Sweden, this does not imply any changes in the ongoing work. The risk assessments and the important strategies and measures presented in recent days remain in place.'[7]

If the virus had been judged to be far away in mid-February, the Public Health Agency had to change its view after the spread of the virus accelerated in northern Italy and Iran. Some measures were introduced in Sweden in early March. On 2 March, the agency updated the risk assessment for COVID-19 cases in Sweden to very high and for a general spread in the country to moderate. A series of recommendations followed:

> [T]esting of people who had travelled in certain Italian regions and certain Alpine regions, such as South Tyrol, and had developed symptoms within 14 days, advice against travelling to northern Italy, expanded COVID-19 testing for all patients who had flu-like symptoms on contact with the health service, cancellation of gatherings of more than 500 people and improved public information. (under the responsibility of the Swedish Civil Contingencies Agency)

A coordination group was created, as 'we have to have a high level of preparedness throughout society and that requires coordination'.[8] This conviction seemed to be global, or at least European, as Hallengren, the Minister for Social Affairs, declared with reference to the work of the EU Council for Employment, Social Policy, Health and Consumer Affairs on COVID-19 and the joint EU procurement of healthcare equipment. The Swedish coordination group included a number of organizations under the leadership of the Public Health Agency: the National Board of Health and Welfare, the Swedish Civil Contingencies Agency, the Swedish Medical Products Agency, the Swedish Agency for Labour and the Swedish Association of Local Authorities and Regions.

On the front line of healthcare, the issue of protective equipment was becoming urgent and was being addressed at European level through coordination and joint procurement. At both local and national level, many public sector organizations struggled with the urgency of the crisis and the bureaucracy of the regulatory framework. Public sector employees needed equipment in the here and now, while the procurement legislation has rules and timeframes for ensuring competition between suppliers, conducting assessments and writing contracts. Exceptions to the timeframe for standard procedures due to the pandemic also needed to be examined. On 1 April 2020, the Official Journal of the European Union stated that

> COVID-19 is a health crisis that requires quick, smart solutions and agility in dealing with a huge increase in demand for similar goods and services, while disrupting some supply chains. Public procurers in Member States are at the forefront of most of these goods and services. They have to ensure the availability of personal protective equipment such as face masks and protective gloves, medical technology products such as ventilators, other emergency medical devices, but also hospital and IT infrastructure, to name just a few examples. (European Commission, 2020: 3)

The EU declared that speedy purchasing of goods and services was to be prioritized over the normal procurement procedure and authorized buyers to negotiate directly with suppliers. While bureaucrats and lawyers tried to resolve the tension between the pandemic emergency and normal public sector procedures, workers had to deal with the crisis in practice. In many places, there was no protective equipment,[9] and so workers looked for quick local solutions.

These could be unusual, off-the-shelf suppliers from 'a whole lot of strange places', as one local government chairman put it (C20, local government chairman, West). A local government manager from the same municipality told us: 'We bought a pallet for 200,000 kronor by chance and it contained a variety of protective coats, visors and breathing masks. We realized that we and many others could be ripped off, but at least 80 per cent was good, so we built up a stock.' When asked where the municipality found all the equipment when there was a general shortage, the head of the municipality replied:

> It was someone they met on LinkedIn who knew someone who knew someone ... In XXX municipality there was a company that dealt in tarpaulins and mattresses and they switched fairly quickly to producing visors. They may not have been the best in the world, but it was something. Then we went down to Biltema and bought all the gloves available. In [X] they started their own apron production, they were cutting plastic. (C19, municipal manager, West)

Local solutions also included in-house production of protective equipment. A committee secretary in a municipality in western Sweden described how visors were manufactured by the municipality's employees at the initiative of the social services administration (C2, municipal board secretary, West). Some municipalities produced visors using 3D printing and others from vacuum cleaner bags. In a municipality in northern Sweden, one of our interviewees testified that

> it was difficult to get hold of face masks and face shields, so [the crisis management committee] started making them themselves and they were heavily criticized. They made masks from vacuum cleaner bags ... and they were approved. The municipality was heavily criticized for that initiative, but we were proactive and we made it work. Then people contacted the people who initiated it. Around the country. 'How did you do it? What did you do?' At first, the newspapers wrote that people had vacuum cleaner bags over their heads. (C3, municipal secretary, North)

In many municipalities, reactions to the in-house production of visors changed over time from criticism to praise. Some of the interviewees who worked in elderly care and had direct contact with the elderly and their relatives told us how their managers initially did not approve of visors and then made them compulsory – after less than a month. One assistant nurse said:

> We decided to make our own visors as the municipality did not provide any protective equipment at all. Our idea was to use them for all care-related activities but to otherwise continue working according to the established procedures – distancing, basic hand hygiene. We were immediately contacted by our manager who told us not to use them.

> That it would be perceived as offensive to our users and that it had been decided higher up that no visors could be used. If someone in the work group was particularly anxious, the manager offered them a counselling session. When we communicated the concerns of relatives and users and the demand for protective equipment, we received no response. (B1, assistant nurse, Central East)

Staff at Central East were forced to contact Kommunal[10] to gain support for the use of visors produced in-house. But the discussion continued for three weeks before the municipality finally introduced a requirement to use visors.

Fighting the virus: from clean hands to keeping a distance and everything in between

The pandemic was a crisis that was initially centred on the health sector, as its severity was expressed in the number of people who were intensely ill and died. At the same time, responsibility for reducing the spread of infection fell on the whole of society. The idea was that everyone could make a difference in the spread of infection and that everyone therefore had a moral duty to contribute – especially when the horrors of the healthcare system began to reach the public. As a deputy director of healthcare in Central East put it, the pandemic was 'initially and, really, all the time ... exciting to be involved in and see how quickly we have been able to adapt', but 'we were terrified because you saw that a lot of people were in ICU, people were dying and what were we supposed to do? How could we contribute to reducing the spread of infection?'

The whole community was called on to act towards a common goal: to slow down, if not stop, the progress of the virus. People made great efforts to keep their distance, wash their hands, stay at home at the sign of the slightest symptom and telecommute, all to ensure that welfare services could continue to be provided. There was also a lot of work involved in ensuring that the recommendations were followed, as well as evidence of social control over the health of colleagues and other people. At universities, it was not long before the first letters from senior managers arrived encouraging frequent and thorough hand washing. Detailed instructions on how to wash hands were also posted in university toilets. A public health coordinator in a municipality in western Sweden told us that there was initially an atmosphere of suspicion, as an allergy, for example, could be confused with a possible COVID sniffle, leading to deteriorating relations in the workplace.

The work that the entire public sector – both within and outside the healthcare system – became involved in to reduce the spread of infection was not without organizational difficulties. One such was that the zero tolerance for 'sniffles at work' together with the increasing number of people infected made staffing a more difficult issue than usual. On their internal websites, some municipalities and authorities posted information about limited material resources and the lack of staff 'in different positions/ workplaces' (B2, food inspector, Central). Municipalities and authorities were concerned not only about people who were particularly vulnerable and fragile but also about not being able to fulfil their mission as part of the public sector when many employees were sick and/or had to stay at home:

> There was concern – partly for the target group we work with, because we work with elderly people who are ill. We didn't know what it would be like, to what extent it would affect the people we meet, how many would die, how many would become seriously ill and how many resources we would need. There was also a fear that ... one of us would fall ill – how we would manage this and at the same time take care of our users, the biggest group that became ill. So there was a lot of anxiety, fears –you would stay at home at the slightest symptom, precisely because we meet the elderly and absolutely did not want to infect them. (D12, care worker, South Central)

Some municipalities worked systematically with staffing scenarios so they could plan what to do if the number of employees off sick was too high:

> Then we made a decision very early on ... to run simulations linked to staffing if 20 per cent were off sick. Then I decided ... you can increase staffing by at least one position per unit, and in the preschool as well. So you had someone extra right from the start. Since we weren't sure whether there would be any [government] subsidies or not, allowing them to increase staffing was a fairly successful decision. (C19, municipal manager, West)

Another difficulty was transforming some of the employees' work tasks into telework, especially in cases where certain vulnerable target groups were dependent on the welfare services that would now be carried out remotely. A social worker at South Central told us:

> We did most of our work on the phone, or via Teams. At the same time, it didn't really work for our target group, where many of them don't have digital skills. So we had to make lots of visits anyway. Physical distancing was important. Sometimes we judged that they couldn't bring a relative, except for those who really needed it and couldn't speak for themselves. But then we kept our distance, which was difficult because many of them have difficulty with hearing, while we had masks

> and visors and sat very far away. Communication difficulties arose pretty quickly, you might say. (D12, assistance officer, South Central)

The caseworker also said they had to strike a compromise between the COVID-19 restrictions and the quality of the meeting with those in need of assistance. Supervisors tried to meet citizens and at the same time contribute to reducing the spread of infection by making the necessary changes in their work tasks. Particular problems arose in contexts where staff worked with confidential documents while sitting at home in their improvised offices and workplaces:

> There was a lot of talk about us working a lot from home. From our point of view, it does not work in the same way as in other places, because we have to be on site and receive the reports that come in; it's all about confidentiality. You can't just send things any old way, it has to be sent by fax to be secure, and someone has to be there on site and receive it. So as far as we were concerned, most people were on site. But there were still some who worked from home, which meant that those of us who were always on site had to do a lot – can you check this, can you look in my box, can you take my mail, can you check it, will you print it out for me? A lot of things like that. (D9, technical administrator, South Central)

Two new groups of workers were created: 'on-site workers' and 'home workers'. The relationship between them could become tense as some of the cases could not be handled fully digitally and therefore required some physical presence in the office. This meant an increased workload for those who remained in their regular workplaces. New solutions were therefore needed to respond to the need or desire to work from home yet not overburden the on-site workers with providing services for the home workers:

> We – that's me and another administrator – said: 'We can't have this! We can't manage these tasks for you because then we won't have time to do what we need to do.' So we had to divide it up in a different way. Those who wanted and felt that they needed – or rather, wanted – to be at home, they had to come here in the evenings or early mornings when no one else was here, and print out their papers and check their mailboxes. Because it's unsustainable in the long run. (D9, technical administrator, South Central)

Although much of the work was transformed into digital work, digitalization was not always unproblematic. One example was found in environmental inspections. Many municipalities enabled inspectors to work from home by sending a questionnaire to restaurants or other businesses due to be inspected, scheduling Teams meetings or asking them to send menus and labels. 'Desktop inspection' seemed to be a new concept for inspectors: 'But it is very difficult to carry out certain inspections. ... And not everyone has a webcam or can participate in that way. ... We have realized that it takes much more time than regular inspections' (C6, environmental manager, North).

In some municipalities, the inspectors continued to work off site only to check closing times: 'Then I have met some restaurateurs who have been open, for takeaways' (C7, environmental and health protection inspector, West). In other municipalities, the inspectors judged that the work could not be done from home: 'Corona supervision of catering establishments. ... I think we have done over a hundred corona inspections' (C4, environmental inspector, North). In the new digitalized or partially digitalized work, many people testified to tensions that were difficult to resolve and also to detect. When we talked to a head of office in Central East, we mentioned the thesis that 'If you don't meet, you have nothing to argue about.' This was the answer:

> It's both. There are two aspects. Yes, as you say, you probably hold back a little more. At the same time, there is a risk that certain things won't come to the surface. Which is actually the root cause. This is the real problem. There is a risk that it becomes a conflict, and we are often scared of conflicts, so then it doesn't come up. So we walk around like a cat on a hot potato. We never get to the bottom of what the problem is. In a face-to-face meeting, you get the chance to see, hear and read the person's whole body language and then say, 'Excuse me, I realize now that you seem to find this difficult. What is it?' I can't read that on the screen at all. I guess that's one thing that I feel is lacking. (B32, chancellery, Central East)

Working remotely brought difficulties in reading social contexts. Several people said it was particularly difficult to read and assess relationships between colleagues when new work constellations were created in response to pandemic management. There was a risk of 'beating around the bush' and with limited opportunities to detect each other's tense behaviour. With regard to social distancing, it became clear that factors such as social class, type of housing and personal (family) situation affected some employees particularly hard. It therefore became important to keep a close eye on colleagues even when working remotely. As a building inspector in the West said, it was 'very important that you talk a lot with each other and keep in touch', as 'you noticed that many colleagues were very lonely and felt very down' (C14, building inspector, West).

Directives from above: help or hindrance?

The tension between the progress of the pandemic and the decision-making processes of the public bureaucracy emerged as a clear theme in our interviews. Interviewees often talked about having different solutions, some successful and others criticized, to manage the crisis and continue to ensure that welfare services worked despite extraordinary circumstances. Many decisions were taken in the name of the pandemic both at local level, in municipalities and regions, and at national level, by the government and various authorities.

The timing of these decisions became a hot topic of discussion: too fast, too slow, too early or too late. As previously reported, some managers were perceived as having been too slow in reacting to the crisis and introducing certain measures, such as mandatory visors in elderly care. In other places, managers were instead too quick. A social worker in South Central told us that the municipality's measures were sometimes agreed and introduced before the government decided on general directives and recommendations (which could sometimes go in the opposite direction), which was interpreted as the municipality's management disrupting operations and removing activities in advance unnecessarily:

> [T]his municipality ... wants to stand out a bit. Before government decisions were made, they were ahead of the game and made local political decisions about things like working from home, not travelling on business and so on. Then there have been national ones as well, but they've been a bit quick here. ... It has caused irritation on these occasions when we've acted early because it has disrupted the activities. ... And it didn't arouse very positive feelings. (D10, social worker, South Central)

The underlying reasons for managers' decisions in state and municipal organizations were also the subject of debate. Leaders in all organizations came up with different measures, which – according to many employees – testified to management's lack of knowledge of what was going on in practice. Many people interpreted rapid changes in decisions as confused and confusing. A library coordinator in a western Swedish municipality said:

> [T]here have been various swings back and forth all the time. There was a bit of panic in the beginning ... They didn't know how to deal with this and how serious it would be. There was talk of total shutdowns even then, but it only happened later, in December. People were very worried. The information was inadequate. There was information at so many levels: the state, the county, municipalities and how they should

> relate to each other when they said different things. There was a lot of uncertainty. (C10, library coordinator, West)

According to this interviewee, the information was not sufficient. As Tegnell had declared, an informed public is part of Swedish crisis preparedness, and therefore the criticism of the lack of information was particularly strong. Communicators and secretaries in the municipalities noticed this, reporting that their workload increased significantly as the number of meetings and decisions increased. Despite their efforts, communication in the municipalities initially suffered from scattered, rapid and often contradictory decisions that came from different directions and at different levels. A principal at a school in South East described problems with communication in the municipality as follows: '[A]t the beginning there was a lot of confusion in the South East. There were very different approaches, you could say. They [those responsible at the municipality] were the ones who sat and waited for a directive, and then they acted' (D14, principal, South East).

Waiting for directives, and the lack of clear rules from above, was experienced in several places. The librarian coordinator in South Central regretted that, in the absence of comprehensive and clear information for both staff and the public, staff had to find their own ways of dealing with encounters with citizens in libraries:

> They wanted the manager to say, 'This is what we're going to do', so that everyone knew, so that one person didn't interpret it one way and someone else another way. I thought that took a bit too long. And then there was a bit of 'it's up to everyone to set their own limits', which I think is difficult in such a context. When you have a social job where you have to help people, in our case visitors, I would have liked more clear directives from above, saying 'This is how we do it.' So that everyone was on the same footing and that I could tell the visitor, 'No, we have these rules.' So that a visitor didn't meet another of my colleagues the next day and get different help that they didn't get from me. It was a bit misleading. (D5, library assistant, South Central)

In many places, the initial sense of confusion caused by multiple decisions and unclear directives led to attempts to coordinate information, decisions and actions within and between different organizations. After the first month of the pandemic, the number of coordination meetings had already increased dramatically, and they came to be perceived as a necessity. A principal in South East reported that 'people began to understand that we had to be coordinated, and so we started a coordination meeting in the municipality with all principals every Friday' and 'in dialogue with our own infection control doctor'. The coordination involved a lot of new work:

> The [infectious diseases doctor] sent information to the administration that they put together in a letter, so all of us headteachers got the same information. Then we had a forum on Fridays, where we all met digitally, and then we could discuss a question that had arisen: how do we handle it? We all did the same thing and I think that was important, otherwise it would have been complete chaos. ... I think it got off the ground fairly quickly in our municipality compared to many other municipalities. (D14, principal, South East)

Different ripples on different ponds: any other problems that arose

As society as a whole struggled to slow or stop the progress of the virus, public sector workers were under increasing pressure to continue to deliver the services for which their organizations were responsible. Their work and efforts led to different consequences in different places, rather like different ripples on different stretches of water. But the different actions often turned out to be affecting organizations in ways that could not have been anticipated at the outset. Examples of such cross effects can be found in municipalities' elderly care and social services.

Elderly care

When the first medical studies in early February 2020 showed that people who were elderly and/or had underlying diseases were most at risk of serious consequences from contracting COVID-19, elderly care quickly became the most talked-about welfare area, both in the political and public debate and in the country's municipalities. 'Protecting the elderly' became the formal objective of the Public Health Agency, the government and the municipal administrations, as was formulated during the first weeks of the pandemic. Direct measures, such as the government's decision on 30 March 2020 to impose a total ban on visits to nursing homes and the agency's report offering recommendations and support for regions, municipalities and providers of care for the elderly (April 2020), together with targeted investments in protective equipment, gave responsible decision makers a toolbox that directly influenced the work in the country's care homes.

Changed hygiene practices when in contact with residents, strict visiting rules, adapted scheduling and staffing are just a few examples of areas where elderly care staff had to adapt their daily work. The direct adaptation and the efforts required by care staff were also recognized both locally, in the country's municipalities and regions, and nationally:

> Anna-Lena Blixth has been nominated by the Ljusdal-Järvsö branch of the Swedish Red Cross and the regional council in Central Sweden for the international award, the Florence Nightingale Medal, a nomination that the Swedish Red Cross then submitted. Anna-Lena has been nominated for her supportive role as the municipality's dementia nurse and for helping to find the right people for the job and the right kind of protective equipment for staff in care homes and home care services. During the ongoing pandemic, the concern has been greater than usual and the pressure on the dementia nurses as a group has increased as they have had to find new ways to manage their tasks and other ways of working in order to fulfil their supportive role. (Ljusdal municipality)[11]

What was less talked about was how the usual work with elderly care was indirectly affected by the focus on COVID-19 patients. Older people with non-COVID illnesses found it more difficult to receive care during the pandemic. Dementia assessments were delayed, and some residents in care homes faced delays:

> [They were] very communicatively ill, so to speak, which led to an urgent need for us. Then cancer care, which like other care was neglected during the pandemic. [This meant] greater responsibility for us as a municipality to solve problems for people who actually needed medical care, but which we would try to solve with nursing care. (D12, social worker, South Central)

Another indirect impact on elderly care work was related to social distancing. As the usual social services, such as childcare and group meetings, were put on hold during the first pandemic period, many older people suffered psychological isolation, ate less and 'quite a few became suicidal' (D12, social worker, South Central). In addition, many family members cut down on their visits due to the risk of infection, thus reducing the 'huge' amount of home care work done by family members, which 'now fell on us. Then we had the home care staff who couldn't get it together because they had to stay at home at the slightest sign of a symptom' (D12, assistance officer, South Central).

Social services

Like the staff in elderly care, those working in social services also faced difficulties in carrying out their tasks, not only as a direct result of the formal restrictions but also because other parts of society changed their ways of working. At the end of March 2020, the National Board of Health and Welfare issued advice to social services, emphasizing that they were a socially important activity and that it was important that this activity continued even during a crisis. Given the restrictions and measures taken in the municipalities, the social services should, as far as possible, continue to plan and implement their mission as required by law.

But the ability to do their job with fewer staff and based on existing hygiene and work procedures was also complicated by clients using their symptoms and the Public Health Agency's recommendations as a tactic to avoid contact with social services by not attending meetings. In the same way as in the past, social workers had to deal with both regular and emergency cases that in some cases required direct intervention. However, this time circumstances were complicated by COVID-19 restrictions and the other recommendations to keep a distance. A social worker at South Central told us:

> [I]t is clear that we must follow the restrictions that exist, and be careful, but if a child is at risk, that must take precedence in the end. But where do we draw the line and when can we demand that people see us, even if they say they can't? So that is also a challenge in this profession. (D10, social worker, South Central)

Staff saw their professional role as socially important and were prepared to fulfil it at all costs:

> [J]ust in case it was a very acute situation where you need to go into a home and make an assessment, we had kits in our backpacks with full protective clothing and gloves. If we needed to go in where we knew there was infection. In order to make a protection assessment, it was important to have as much protective equipment as possible. And easy access to it ... we couldn't say, 'No, we can't meet the families now.' It was never the case that the board or anyone else said that it was okay to extend investigation times. Instead, we had to do what we usually do, so that's what we had to do. (D10, social worker, South Central)

These brief examples from elderly care and social services represent only a small part of the state and municipal organizations where the indirect effects of the pandemic measures were expressed. In later chapters of the book, we show how both intended and more unexpected consequences of the pandemic response affected Sweden's schools, libraries and courts.

The first part of pandemic management: a lot of organization, confusion and urgency

Despite some media attention from January 2020 and several announcements from the WHO and the Public Health Agency, the arrival of the pandemic in Sweden in March 2020 came as a surprise to many. The situation became acute and resulted in various recommendations, directives and decisions being made by the government, authorities, regions and municipalities to reduce the spread of infection. This plethora of decisions was confusing for many but was justified by others by the Swedish principle of responsibility:

> Unlike in many other countries, the Swedish administrative model is based on the principle of responsibility, which means that the responsibilities of the authorities remain with the support of experts even during crises. The model is a practical way to prevent various forms of (politically motivated) abuse of power in a living democracy. Authorities are thus entitled to a certain degree of self-determination regarding the best interests of citizens. (B14, university lecturer, Central)

The Swedish model also made it clear that the public sector could decide and act in different ways in different parts of the country, depending on their own interpretation of the recommendations and on the local situation.

In practice, however, the public sector was put in a difficult position, as it was expected to act relatively independently to quickly stop the pandemic while maintaining normal bureaucratic decision-making processes. Society as a whole had to be engaged against the invisible enemy while maintaining and safeguarding the democratic organization of welfare. This also meant that municipalities and state authorities had to reorganize many of their activities in order for the public sector to continue to fulfil its function. It is in connection with this that the expression 'knee-jerk reorganization' was most frequently used:

> We had to reorganize a lot, move all the desks apart [to get] distance between the desks instead of seating groups. We had to have soap, paper towels and hand sanitizer in every classroom. We had to empty one student room to give us two canteens, and we also had to empty the school library. In two days it was ready. ... Scheduling was also tricky. (C8, principal, West)

In the early months, it was the sense of some kind of crisis exception that forced unusual organization of public services. But after all this effort, things would soon return to normal. The head of social services in South Central expressed this in the following way:

> We probably thought that the pandemic would end by April, maybe May, and then it would be business as usual. But the groundwork we did that spring has been sustained throughout the pandemic. So we have been more prepared for the other waves and just watched: 'Okay, is there anything we should change here, or should we work as before?' So it's more about reconsidering certain parts when the other waves have come and if something has looked a little different. (D7, social services manager, South Central)

But the road to 'the new normal' took several months ...

4

The New, the Old and the New Old

After the summer, many people returned to quieter work and quieter workplaces. The spread of infection remained low in the early autumn; the new ways of working had become routines. Digital meetings, less travel, more working from home – all this remained but had taken on a more efficient form; meetings became shorter, and people learned to use digital tools. By mid-autumn, there was hope that the pandemic might be coming to an end, as the pharmaceutical industry, the Public Health Agency of Sweden and the government started talking about preparations for mass vaccination of the Swedish population. Few suspected, however, that the calm that emerged during the summer and early autumn of 2020 was simply the calm before the storm:

> The key word of the period was 'adaptation', although small absurdities continued: recommendations were constantly changing, it was not possible to fulfil certificate requirements, and so on. (B23, family counsellor, Central East)

> This amazing ability that we humans have: we adapt! It feels a bit strange at first, but then it's not so strange. (B29, family counsellor, Central East)

> I think we adapt a lot, we cultural workers, or those of us in libraries anyway, but we always adapt to the situation. (D5, library assistant, South Central)

As the spring weather improved and summer approached, so did the hope of spending more time outdoors. The spread of infection decreased during the summer of 2020, and many people spent their holidays pursuing outdoor activities but continuing to wash their hands and keep their distance. A new word was established in our vocabulary: *hemester*, a combination of 'home' (in Swedish *hemma*) and 'vacation' (in Swedish *semester*).

A survey conducted by the Public Health Agency and published in June 2020 showed that 'an estimated 0.9 per cent of the population had an ongoing SARS CoV-2 upper respiratory tract infection between 21 and 24 April and 0.3 per cent between 25 and 28 May' (Public Health Agency, 2020b). The infection rate even went down in Region Stockholm, which had always had a higher rate than the rest of the country. Between 21 and 24 April, 2.3 per cent of Stockholm residents had an ongoing COVID-19 infection, while during the period 25–28 May the figure was 0.7 per cent.

How the Swedish public sector dealt with the pandemic in the spring and early summer of 2020 was largely linked to the spread of infection. Little seemed to be done in terms of long-term efforts and preparations, and most of the day-to-day activities of Swedish state authorities and municipalities were focused on coping with everyday life. In fact, this period can be described in three key themes. First, the pandemic measures and their effects began to be evaluated, mainly by comparing various aspects of public health before and after the pandemic. Second, it became apparent that the media-driven public debate was beginning not only to seriously scrutinize the situation but, frequently, to challenge the authorities' handling of the pandemic. Third, the differences in perception of the pandemic and its consequences became very visible, at least in our interviews.

Comparison with the first period: reduced transmission and better health?

In what we call the second period of pandemic management, public organizations – and indeed society as a whole – began to be seen by politicians, the media and academics as adapting to pandemic-related measures relatively well. This image was both created and reinforced by positive figures showing a reduction in the spread of infection and by an increasing number of studies that more systematically compared the interventions and measures between the different phases of the pandemic. For example, the Public Health Agency published several studies that presented not only the actual spread of infection divided by different demographic aspects but also the behaviour of various sections of the population in different contexts.

A study published in June 2020 analysed behaviours and concerns in reaction to information dissemination, concluding that 'the majority have listened to the authorities' recommendations during the spring' (Public Health Agency, 2020c). During week 11 (mid-March), that is, just after COVID-19 had been declared a pandemic, 'almost 6 out of 10 persons had adjusted their everyday life to the new requirements, and from week 13 onwards 8 out of 10 had adapted their everyday life due to the coronavirus'

(Public Health Agency, 2020c). This level of adaptation was sustained, according to the agency, which led them to conclude that 'a large majority have followed the Agency's recommendations over a long period of time and have maintained adaptation and stayed informed'. The study showed that people were even more willing to practise hand hygiene, avoid crowds, keep their distance and avoid visiting the elderly.

These positive results were nevertheless interpreted in different ways. On the one hand, the Public Health Agency could point to the fact that the proposed measures and recommendations, combined with the willingness of the Swedish people to follow them, had produced results. On the other hand, the warmer spring and summer weather helped to increase outdoor activities and socializing. Yet since people generally responded that they followed recommendations on keeping their distance, practising hand hygiene and avoiding crowds, the agency could interpret results of different surveys to mean that the measures taken had made a difference, and that Sweden's 'strong tradition of volunteerism with an emphasis on individual responsibility' was working.

To better understand the effects of the pandemic, we made comparisons with previous years, and with other infections. Several of our interviewees said that Swedish people in general had become healthier due to better hygiene and greater distancing, which contributed to a decrease in the spread of infections. The Public Health Agency confirmed in a study that the sale of antibiotics for respiratory infections had decreased, '[p]erhaps due to the reduction in the number of infections'. The spread of diseases other than COVID-19 also decreased because of the COVID-19 recommendations. For example, the influenza season peaked in week 10 (before COVID-19 was declared a pandemic) and ended in week 13, which was 'the fastest closure seen in the last 20 years of influenza surveillance' (Public Health Agency, 2020c).

Other positive effects could also be discerned during this period. The strains of spring seemed to bring people working in public services closer together, and they showed greater understanding and care for each other. Our interviewees suggested that 'people have become nicer to each other' (B29, family counsellor, Central East), and that they 'talked to each other more' (B30, education manager, Central). But not always, and not everywhere.

The experience of the spring left its mark on the way in which many people started to perceive their jobs and their workplaces. There were concerns about the long-term health consequences of the pandemic and its management. Many of our interviewees also pointed out that social distancing, the lack of physical proximity and even working from home could contribute to poorer mental health. As an employment officer explained to us: 'Social distancing is possible, but it is stressful; it's stressful not being able to hug someone and be close' (B20, employment officer, Central North).

It seemed to be particularly stressful for management staff, as they were not used to their employees not being physically at their workplaces. As one municipal manager put it: 'It isn't the same, going around and talking to each other in the morning, picking up on moods and so on' (C19, municipal manager, West).

Working from home also made it difficult to maintain the customary boundaries between work and private life. These boundaries are usually maintained physically, through the obvious physical difference between a delimited workplace and a home where family and personal life take place. Now these boundaries had to be invented and enforced at home. Many interviewees told us that it took them a few months to learn to navigate these new boundaries. As one business coordinator put it, they 'had to learn how to manage the relative freedom of work ... [and] how to feel free when you are at home' (B17, business coordinator, Central).

The discussion about possible consequences for public health, other than the direct COVID-19 infection, was also picked up by the Public Health Agency, which had already published a report on the subject in June 2020 (Public Health Agency, 2020d). The report, which could be read as an experience-based publication rather than a new study, listed several risk areas within the public health policy goals that might be negatively affected by the pan-European pandemic (they called them 'the indirect consequences for health'). They highlighted the risk that public health would become more unequal between different social and demographic groups. This perception of the effects of the pandemic as being unequally distributed was also central to our interviewees and often recurred in their reflections on the second period of the pandemic.

Mediatization: between the colourful drama and the greyness of everyday

As mentioned in the previous chapter, the pandemic became a favourite topic for the established media, as well as for social media and alternative information channels. In Sweden, as in the global arena, information dissemination was identified early on as an important tool for raising awareness of the pandemic. The Swedish public health and governance model – mentioned in previous chapters and often repeated and emphasized by Public Health Agency representatives at their daily conferences – was a central component of pandemic management. The model has personal responsibility as its basis: it formulates recommendations to citizens, and it takes for granted the duty of a clear and effective dissemination of information and the constant utilization of the data provided by the authorities.

That the pandemic became a major theme in the media not only meant that the media reported the daily number of deaths, hospitalizations and infections. To a large extent, the way the pandemic was presented, how it was interpreted and how its handling was described followed the media logic, with its focus on dramatization of both form and content. The media not only reported on the pandemic but also created dramas, for example around conflicts between different scientists and research groups, between countries and their different strategies and between social groups that could be pitted against each other on issues such as the closure of some businesses but not others, travel restrictions, limitations on public transport or tax breaks for certain industries.

This 'mediatization' became particularly noticeable during the second period of the pandemic. In our conversations with other researchers, we often heard them mention mediatization's positive effects, such as better exposure of research results, an increase in research funding and growing public engagement in scientific issues and debates. But the media-driven debate also had negative aspects. One researcher argued that 'the media discourages rather than informs' (B22, Central East), not least because of the polarization of views that journalists often sought to create or reinforce. Some claimed there was a 'lynch mob atmosphere'. For example, there was much mention of virology, a subject that few general readers were familiar with, so that it was difficult for the public to know whom and what to believe. In such a context, media coverage could create highly charged conflicts between different research groups on such issues as how the virus worked, how it affected our bodies and how best to protect ourselves:

> They sought the edge of conflict all the time. And they pushed this edge of conflict until it really did become a conflict. But it was not about the big numbers, the big picture. It could be about a single figure here or there. I think this was actually a very nasty process ... then we got this guillotine that completely strikes right through the research community in a way, when some researchers become outcasts, while others are still in the family. (B27, communication advisor, Centre)

Such polarization of opinions and the media dramas were also embedded in many stories explaining how the entire public sector in Sweden should respond to the pandemic. At times, it was difficult for public authority staff and municipal employees to navigate the public debate and to find ways to manage the pandemic within the framework of their activities without risking being exposed to media scrutiny and criticism. This was especially true for major decisions that had to be taken quickly. The effects and scope of such decisions were not based on any previous experience; they were not 'business as usual'. Conflicts had occurred and difficult decisions had been made in the past, but now '[i]n the midst of conflicts and stuff and "working miracles" comes corona' (B19, museum line manager, West South). The media coverage was therefore particularly stressful when municipalities and authorities needed to ensure that the social infrastructure continued to function. A municipal secretary in North felt sorry for her more exposed colleagues who could fall victim to what she perceived as unfair or scandalous media coverage:

> You shouldn't listen to the media so much. For example, the North municipality was [described] negatively in the media many times and the picture was so wrong. It's important that they [the media] exist, but sometimes they just want headlines, which is sad, because we have done a tremendous job. People have committed themselves 1,000 per cent and done their utmost, and this is followed by near ridicule in the media. I think that's disgraceful. The media needs to think and check the facts. Check with sources before throwing out headlines. (C3, municipal secretary, North)

The sense of vulnerability associated with the public and media debate was also reinforced by the ways in which public sector actions were described in social media. There, the public expressed their support for the 'heroes of welfare' (mainly in healthcare and education), but they also directed threats and harassment at public employees – researchers, politicians and government representatives. A new word emerged: infodemic. Launched by journalist David Rothkopf in a *Washington Post* column during the 2003 SARS epidemic, the word was re-used by the World Health Organization's Director-General at a meeting of foreign policy and security experts in Germany in mid-February 2020. He said: 'We're not just fighting an epidemic; we're fighting an infodemic.'[1]

The accelerating pace of social media and news flows made managing the infodemic even more difficult. As one teacher put it:

> The media have blown this up. Ten years ago, it wouldn't have been so widespread. We would have become ill and died, but it would not have been described the same way as it is now. There's almost a competition to be seen as the worst ... My old mum is following this because she has nothing else to do. (C17, teacher, West)

In different areas of the public sector, one could see signs that the pandemic actually only reinforced a phenomenon that had existed for a long time, but which now became truly visible, namely that social media are an important part of how public organizations and their employees interpret and design their work and adapt it to norms that govern media coverage (Eriksson-Zetterquist and Pallas, 2022).

Not the same pandemic for all

The expression 'the new normal' began to establish itself, and several of our interviewees said that it was, after all, 'business as usual' (B23, family counsellor, Central East) and that they were back to 'a grey everyday life' (B25, healthcare project manager, Central East). A municipal secretary in North municipality confirmed that while the first period was characterized by improvisation, 'quite quickly we felt that we needed to get a routine for this. We were quick to establish routines' (C3, municipal secretary, North); after all, routines and decisions are common organizational tools in the public sector.

In this second period, public sector workers began to recognize differences in both how the pandemic was experienced and how it was managed by different professional groups and in different parts of the country. Diaries and interviews revealed large differences in working conditions within seemingly similar professions, such as researchers and journalists, but also between Swedish citizens and asylum seekers, between permanent and temporary staff and between urban and rural residents. As one researcher who had a second job in the cultural sector said:

> Those of us in culture have basically just been shut down. People often forget about us 'hourly workers' in such situations, even though we are central to the daily functioning of organizations. We stand at the cash register, we guide the visitors, we give instructions, we check tickets, we stand in the middle of the shop, of the restaurant, of the cloakroom – but are just as easy to get rid of as we are to call in. (B4, researcher, Central)

Even within the health sector, where staff had been widely celebrated, the interviewees said there were large differences between those who were seen as heroes and those who had less visible roles. One project leader explained that it was common to assume

> that the carers are the heroes and the others are just bystanders. And everybody who is not in direct contact with the patients is administration, even if a nurse is also an administrator when they sit and plan care sessions. But that's not how they see themselves; they see themselves as something else. And then it's often the case that the nurse who plans care visits may not do it quite efficiently, and that it should be someone else, an administratively trained person who does it. (B25, healthcare project manager, Central East)

Feeling both over-used and under-appreciated, the union came to demand better wages in the summer of 2020. As one nurse said: 'This is our year'

(B28, nurse, Central East). Also, it became obvious that how the pandemic was managed was influenced by the size of organizations. Small organizations were able to adapt more easily. University lecturers, for example, compared their experience with that of teachers in smaller colleges, who seemed to adapt more easily to the pandemic than those in large universities, despite the differences in resources and previous experience of distance learning. Comparisons between large cities and small municipalities revealed the same trend:

> I think it's easier to be loyal to your co-workers and stand up for your rights in a smaller municipality. Because you feel more personal responsibility, you know that what you do matters. If you are in Stockholm, you might think, 'What I do doesn't matter, there are so many others who can do it.' So I believe there is a huge difference between small and big municipalities. (C7, environmental and health protection inspector, West)

> [O]ur strength is that we are small and fast! (C9, IT manager, West)

But there were also advantages to being a larger municipality. At least, that is what several of our interviewees claimed when they were asked how things were done in large municipalities. In the metropolitan regions, there was, among other things, greater access to qualified extra staff: 'I know that the town hall made an inventory of nursing staff at an early stage in order to be able to reinforce the health service in case there was a shortage. They pulled all the strings. That is not so easy in a small municipality' (C7, environment and health protection inspector, West).

There was also a difference in the way people living in urban and rural areas experienced the pandemic. In cities with a high population density, it was necessary and more important to follow recommendations, while in rural areas, recommendations were sometimes perceived as difficult to understand and even irrelevant. As one interviewee pointed out, many authorities are located in Stockholm, and it is from there that recommendations are developed. A public health coordinator living in a rural area quoted a conversation with her daughter who lives in Gothenburg:

> She called me and said: 'I think you [in a small municipality] are so nonchalant! You just go to work as if nothing had happened! But I get in my car in the middle of nowhere, drive to the office and park, and walk to work. There are ten people there who represent the danger I expose myself to. I might meet some other people when I go to the food store. Then it's back home and socializing only with my immediate circle of friends. I feel pretty safe. What does your day look like?' 'Just

> like normal, I take public transport, go to the university and then go to the pub. Why do you ask?' (C12, public health coordinator, West)

In many ways, rural life was already moulded to avoid crowds and keep social contacts to a minimum. A building inspector from a rural municipality in West illustrated this clearly:

> Those of us who live in sparsely populated areas find it much easier to adapt to not being in crowds, because there are no crowds here. There are also no restaurants that are open after six o'clock in the evening, so you don't have that problem either. When it comes to public transport, there are two buses that I can take in the morning, and then they go back in the afternoon. And hardly anyone but the children takes the bus, because it doesn't fit with the working times. (C14, building inspector, West)

The calm before the new storm

After the summer, many people returned to quieter work, and to quieter workplaces. The spread of infection remained low in the early autumn, and the new ways of working had become routine; the new normal. Digital meetings, less travelling, more working from home – all this remained but was used in a more efficient way: meetings had become shorter, and people had learnt to use digital tools. 'By June 2020, 80–100 per cent of those who were working had COVID, in September it was only 25 per cent' (B31, deputy director of healthcare, Central East). Managers and employees had learnt to act partly outside formal rules and structures. Public sector managers had to rely on their subordinates doing the right thing without being monitored and scrutinized. Work became 'trust-based', as they started to call it, because there were fewer opportunities to monitor: 'I have decided to work more trust-based, and I feel that the organization as a whole is doing the same. We have to find new [communication] channels. We know that email is not a good way to encourage independent work' (B32, chancellery, Central East).

Several interviewees told us they had gained a better understanding of each other's problems, and that many digital challenges – technical, organizational and personal – were being solved more quickly than before. As the head of office at Central East explained:

> We realized that we had too little bandwidth to cope with tasks that depended on fast and reliable connectivity ... It took two weeks of chaos before IT resolved the problem – they didn't expect so many people to use it. So, yes, it has been put to work … which would have taken five years otherwise. (B32, chancellery, Central East)

A little ray of hope showed up in mid-autumn: a hope that the pandemic might be coming to an end, as the pharmaceutical industry, the Public Health Agency and the government started talking about preparations for mass vaccination. Yet very few suspected the storm would come after the calm that had unfolded during the summer.

5

Working in the New Normal

After a summer filled with hope and dedicated to new holiday habits, and an early autumn with new forms of teleworking and improved hand hygiene, the spread of infection returned. Sweden, as well as other European countries, slid straight into the second wave of the pandemic. As the government wrote in its November 2020 Vaccine Proposal, the past summer had been 'in a late pandemic phase with less spread of infection than in the spring. However, in many countries, including Sweden, the spread of infection has increased again since the beginning of the autumn and also leads to an increased number of hospital admissions and deaths' (Government Bill 2020/21:47, p 6 – see Figure 5.1).

With the continued spread of the virus and the first confirmed cases of re-infection in August 2020, it became clear that the fight against COVID-19 could not be won with 'herd immunity' alone. Vaccination now became the most common response to the pandemic, and the desire for an effective vaccine would colour the rest of 2020. But there was also room to summarize and reflect on measures and initiatives implemented within both local and national welfare services.

Summarizing the autumn

Both the media and employees in the public sector looked back on the past six months. The debate on whether the Swedish strategy was good or bad was still lively, and the government initiated several evaluations of the effects of the pandemic and its management. A study of the consequences of teleworking on work environments was assigned to the Swedish Agency for Work Environment Expertise. They concluded that there were many deficiencies in the preparedness of companies, state authorities and municipalities for new forms of work, including increased workload and stress, but there was also the potential to develop and streamline the activities of private and public organizations (Swedish Agency for Work Environment Expertise, 2021: 2).

Figure 5.1: COVID-19 death toll in the autumn of 2020 (week 40: 28 September–4 October)

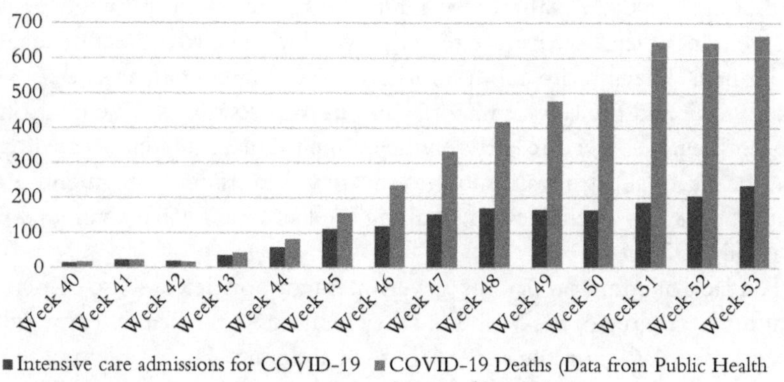

The government appointed special investigators to study the consequences of the pandemic in different sectors. The 'Restarting culture' directive (SOU, 2021:77, p 3) stated that 'in the light of the COVID-19 pandemic, the consequences of the pandemic for the cultural sector should be summarized and the lessons that can be drawn from them analysed'. The inquiry noted both structural and cultural obstacles that threatened to weaken the sector's ability to fulfil its mission and risked undermining opportunities to participate in cultural life and the position of culture in society. The inquiry also concluded that the pandemic had negative consequences for those working in the cultural sector. The transition to digital working methods and deteriorating economic conditions were highlighted as contributing to the generally gloomy picture of the cultural sector (SOU, 2021: 77). In addition to these investigations and assignments, the Corona Commission also worked to evaluate Sweden's strategy against the pandemic. The first interim report was published on 15 December 2020 and dealt with elderly care during the pandemic.

In its introduction, the commission wrote:

> By the beginning of December 2020, more than 7,000 people in Sweden had died with a diagnosis of COVID-19. Of these, almost 90 per cent were aged 70 or older. Half of them were living in special housing and just under 30 per cent had home help. The high proportion of deaths among the frail elderly is in line with the situation in many other countries. We can conclude that the single most important factor behind the large spread of infection and the high number of deaths in elderly care is most likely the general spread of infection in society. (SOU, 2020:10a: 13)

The commission judged that 'the ambition of the Swedish comprehensive strategy to protect the elderly in particular was and is correct', and that 'in comparison with other countries, Sweden is not alone in the high number of deaths in elderly care', which was mainly influenced by the spread of other viruses in the elderly community. Despite this, the commission judged that the element of the Swedish strategy that was intended to protect the elderly had failed. The interim report criticized the fragmented organization of elderly care and the lack of material and human resources. The division of the work with elderly care between the municipal management of care homes and the regional organization of healthcare was considered fragmented and inappropriate, as 'each decision-making level and interface is a vulnerability in itself' (2020: 14).

The lack of attention paid by government authorities was also criticized, as at the beginning of the pandemic they focused on the health sector, while elderly care was left in the shadow of the pandemic. The problem with this 'shadow', according to the commission, was that elderly care organizations lacked leadership, especially in relation to medical expertise. As a result, mortality rates in elderly care were already high in the spring of 2020.

Our study shows that, in the early stages of the pandemic, managers in all parts of the public sector had difficulty leading their organizations and finding their roles, while the professionals found solutions and managed the situation – often despite management's late, and sometimes poor, decisions. In a highly 'managerialized public sector', it was no surprise that the Corona Commission called for more professional governance as a solution.

Longing for the end of autumn

The COVID-19 vaccine became the focus of the media and political spotlight in the autumn of 2020. There was a feeling of hope that the vaccine would put an end to the pandemic. Projects to develop vaccines had been launched all over the world, and by the end of the autumn there were 240 vaccine development projects, 40 of which had entered the clinical phase (Government Bill 2020/21:47). In October 2020, European Commission President Ursula von der Leyen announced that the European Medicines Agency would approve the first vaccines in early December. The speed of the vaccine development was often mentioned in descriptions of these projects, as was the ambiguity and uncertainty about the level of protection achieved and the potential side effects of the vaccine. Memories of Pandemrix, the avian flu vaccine delivered in 2009–10, which is believed to have caused over 400 cases of narcolepsy in Sweden, were once again brought to life.

Sweden received its first shipment of a vaccine in the second half of December, taking delivery of 9,750 doses before Christmas, with a further 80,000 doses arriving the following week. At a press conference on 22 December 2020, the government promised that the vaccination programme would start by 27 December. At the press conference, Hallengren, the Minister for Social Affairs, said:

> As supply increases, more and more people will be vaccinated. The joint goal of the government and the Swedish Association of Local Authorities and Regions is that everyone over the age of 18 and everyone under the age of 18 who is in a risk group will have been offered a vaccine during the first half of 2021. (Social Ministry, 2020)

On the floor: adaptations of the adaptations

Our interviewees told us that while work in the public sector continued more or less as before during the autumn, the routines developed during the spring and summer had to be developed and adapted to this new phase of the pandemic. One municipal secretary described the autumn of 2020 and the following winter as very long: 'Because it just went on and new variants came and then we realized that we would have to learn to live with this' (C3, municipal secretary, North). Several of our interlocutors felt that some initial solutions were no longer appropriate and that new and updated routines and working methods were needed. One primary school teacher told us about his difficulties in following the 'old solutions':

> At the beginning of the autumn, I thought a little more about keeping my distance from the children. But if little Kalle comes in with a cut because he fell in the forest, I can't use pliers to apply the plaster. That would be callous. I have not been able to follow the restrictions as intended ... Children need physical contact sometimes. (C13, teacher, West)

As several teachers pointed out, an adaptation of some COVID measures was necessary because they judged that other needs should be prioritized in certain situations. This might be a child who needed proximity, or the fact that children were not considered to benefit from long periods of physical distancing, or that some subjects could not be taught remotely. This was the case in many practical subjects, such as art courses at university level or chemistry and maths labs in schools. The teacher from the West continued:

> I think it has been the right decision to keep the school open, and at the same time it has been possible to have lessons remotely where necessary. Like the every other day system, because it doesn't work very well to have the seventh graders at home for four weeks ... My colleagues have found it difficult to implement practical elements: chemistry or maths labs are not possible. You have to do it on site. What I would

> have liked was to know what to do with the students who have lost a lot because they had a high level of absence ... What do you do with them? Should they be penalized and made to repeat the class? Or should you offer them an extended school day? Work during holidays? Something that might come afterwards. (C13, teacher, West)

Despite adjustments to the new working practices and despite the 'adaptation of adaptations', many problems remained due to the uncertainty of how staff should handle some of their tasks. In the school world, these difficulties might arise in dealing with pupils who had fallen behind. In some municipalities, the use of solutions from the spring – such as needs assessments, which in some cases had to take place on site – caused confusion during the escalating spread of infection in the autumn.

The adaptation of adaptations sometimes also involved new ways of valuing work practices and the organization's own organization. The ability to manage the pandemic improved as knowledge of the virus, its spread and its effects increased. It seemed possible to adapt parts of the activities in order to keep a distance, such as the relationship with the children and parents in the school, but at times it was easy to forget to consider, for example, the (im)possibility of keeping a distance among the staff. One teacher explained how the adaptation in their school developed during the autumn:

> It was said for a very long time that children do not infect anyone and that children do not get sick. It has since turned out that this may not really be true. I think the school also found it very difficult to understand how it should handle this because we didn't know what it was. We were supposed to keep our distance, but because we were so determined to deal with this in relation to pupils and parents, we were supposed to meet every morning in the staff room, the entire staff, to get an overview of the current situation. So instead of spreading ourselves out more, we met every day. We would never do that now, but we didn't know and didn't understand then. ... We didn't switch to digital meetings until the autumn term. We struggled for quite some time. ... But in the autumn, all the meetings between all staff and within the work unit were digital. (C18, teacher, Central East)

The spread of COVID culminated at the turn of 2020/21: 'There was infection in the spring [2020] and then it died out in the summer so we thought it was over, but then it came back in the autumn and spread everywhere. ... The worst time was in the winter [2020/21] before the vaccination programme started' (C19, municipal manager, West).

As one public health coordinator put it: 'After Christmas everything crashed' (C12, public health coordinator, West). There was a long wait for the vaccine to reach a large part of the population. The peak of the infection was also the reason why the 'new practices' established in the spring of 2020 were followed by even stricter measures, at least in places where the first wave of the pandemic was not as dramatic as in other parts of the country. West was one such municipality, where the late autumn of 2020 put a great strain on most of the municipality's activities:

> Before Christmas, our municipality did its own thing, that was stricter than what the Public Health Agency had said. If someone in the family had the slightest cold, employees in the municipality would stay at home. Then we had to close for a few days because there was no staff because a relative had a cold and needed to be tested. But it was rarely anything. Many people were at home and you ran around with materials, serviced parents, and then you had to help the poor substitute coordinator to think of solutions. It came in spurts ... But I work at a good school where we are there for each other. We're good at helping each other and that makes things easier. (C16, primary school teacher, West)

Many decisions in the municipality during this period were simply taken too quickly and could lead to negative consequences. Libraries were an example of where the measures failed:

> [A]fter this press conference on 18 December 2020, when Mr Löfven [the Prime Minister] said, 'Don't go to the library', all of Sweden's libraries closed down in panic. But, quite quickly, the government was made aware of the fact that libraries are required by law to be open and accessible to all. And then many libraries interpreted this as reopening with restrictions. (D3, library coordinator, South Central)

However, as mentioned earlier, the interpretation of the pandemic's travel restrictions was stricter in some places, and the possibility of keeping libraries open even with restrictions was more limited. In South, the library remained closed:

> We were closed from 18 December 2020 to mid-May 2021. Completely closed for one month, not allowed to give out books, nothing at all, from 18 December until the end of January. After that, we were allowed to start issuing books that had been reserved so our borrowers could pick them up. However, during this entire period – including the autumn – you could not use computers in the library, print out, copy or read newspapers. People were not allowed to sit in the library during that period. So it meant that a lot of the library's mission, which

> is to be accessible to everyone, and our democratic mission to provide information, was limited. (D3, library coordinator, South Central)

During such adaptations and difficulties in performing their work, many staff compared their situation to other parts of the public sector that were having a harder time. The library coordinator, for example, went on to explain that library staff had not been particularly hard hit, but his thoughts went to schools, where 'you worry about' the entire organization of both teachers and pupils. Many people thought of the health service and its heroes, or the elderly care sector, which had been hit really hard:

> I certainly haven't worn myself out like, for example, the people who work in healthcare. There are such contrasts, and I think this has also meant that one group is better off, spending more time with the family and having a good time. Another group wear themselves out, the adults lose their jobs, the children don't go to school, a home is under pressure. It feels like we're almost more polarized after this year. And we must relate to it. (C12, public health coordinator, West)

Management vs professions

A recurring theme in our interviews was the relationship between the role and work of management and the professions. At the beginning of the pandemic, a greater space seemed to have been created for the professions, which were able to handle everyday work in the midst of an acute crisis and despite the management's mistakes. A year later, management had caught up, written guidelines and made decisions, while the Corona Commission had highlighted the need for both better management and professional governance during a crisis. A social services manager told us:

> But information and communication – so that everyone knows what to do – was probably the biggest challenge. And I wasn't alone, we had a medical nurse who did a lot of work when it came to routines and guidelines and had contact with infection prevention in Region Scania, and our hygiene was a big responsibility for her. But she also wanted our backing. Even though she is in a neutral position and has a full mandate, she still wanted us to do these things together, so that it would be good for everyone. Collaboration was also extremely important to make sure that we were sending out the same information and the same message. (D7, social services manager, Central East)

Information and communication remain central during a crisis, and as the social services manager said, collaboration was 'hugely important' for managers. As large parts of the management staff at government agencies and municipalities had difficulty gaining an overview and managing their activities in a more traditional sense at the beginning of the pandemic – partly because remote work did not allow direct insight into what employees were doing – the management discourse often shifted from exercising control to advocating trust-based collaboration. But this did not mean that collaboration increased in all situations. One municipal manager also talked about 'municipal management in new times':

> Leading while not being there can be a problem. That was the most important issue, a new way of making decisions. Normally in a municipality, we have governance, decisions, anchoring and implementation. There are long cycles in most cases, but here it was a matter of when new directives from infection control came in one afternoon, they should apply the following morning. This meant that the managers had to think in a different way. I tried to explain that this was a new situation, you must not hesitate but decide quickly. We also had problems with the union ... Some issues that were previously perhaps a matter for cooperation now had to be decided directly. This applied to Kommunal in particular; it is all about the work environment, the most burning issue. Then we did some training with the managers as well. We had simple exercises and action plans. What happens if there is an infection, for example? ... In home care, someone coughs and then at noon four or six people are coughing. The next day there are this many, and then they had to think, what do we do now? They had read the action plan, but it was a way of practising. (C19, municipal manager, West)

This municipal manager explained that some decisions had to be made quickly and therefore could not become 'a collaboration issue' as before. However, other decisions and workflows had to be more strongly anchored and still required collaboration, such as the aforementioned information and communication flow.

New variations, new waves and summer again

At the start of 2021, it became clear that the pandemic would continue and that it would take a long time for the vaccination programme to slow the progress of the virus. The spread of infection continued until the end of April, but at the same time more groups of the population were vaccinated (see Figure 5.2). However, with the vaccine came a new concern regarding communication: how could information about the vaccine be disseminated to everyone, and what was the best way to counter disinformation about the

Figure 5.2: COVID-19 death toll January–May 2021

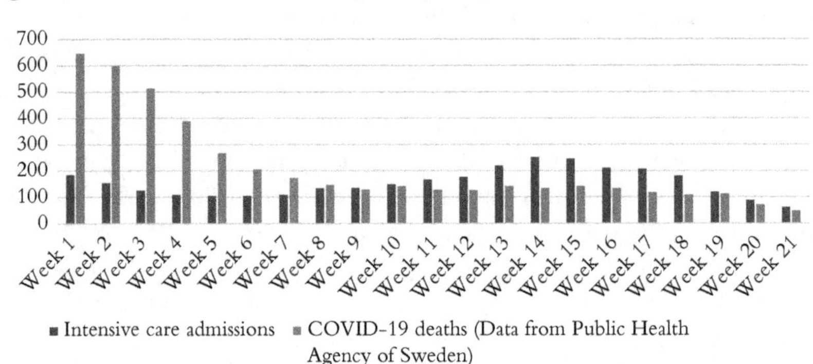

vaccine? The public discourse under the slogan 'We are in the fight against the virus together' applied not only at the beginning of the pandemic, when measures were presented, but also when the vaccine arrived.

Towards the end of the spring, the situation looked a bit brighter than before, as the spread of the virus seemed to be decreasing, and many people had been vaccinated. At the same time, the pandemic had taught public sector employees that developments could be unpredictable and that they should be prepared for new twists and turns and new adaptations. As can be seen in our material from 2021, interviewees were mainly thinking about what they had learnt during the year and what would remain after the pandemic. These questions can best be illustrated through separate themes, and no longer by following the chronological development of the pandemic. But, before presenting the most prominent themes, let us first look at how our study's participants perceived and commented on what we see as the (hopefully) final period of the pandemic.

6

The Pandemic Comes in Waves

The final period of the pandemic in Sweden ran from the summer of 2021 to the summer of 2022. This may seem like a long time, but, after one and a half year of adaptations and readaptations, the employees in the public sector did not need to engage substantively in new procedures or work processes. Beyond the public sector, this period was characterized by reflections on the long-term effects of the pandemic and, as in the previous period, Sweden's response to it. In this chapter, we first present the discussions on the long-term effects of COVID-19 on society in more general terms. We then return to our interviewees' reflections on the cyclical development of the pandemic and their lessons learnt, and their relief that the pandemic seemed to be approaching its final phase.

The long-term effects

In October 2021, the Corona Commission published its first interim report, which evaluated the spread and control of infection in Sweden, as well as the Swedish healthcare and public health system. The commission found that Sweden's response to the pandemic had been characterized by 'tardiness' and initially by 'insufficient' measures, due in part to a lack of legislation and in part to fragmented organization of infection control was fragmented, and that 'it was unclear who was responsible for the whole picture when a serious infectious disease hit the country'. The commission also emphasized that the rapid and challenging transformation of the healthcare system was, above all, 'thanks to the efforts of the employees', and that 'we will live with the consequences of the pandemic for a long time to come' (SOU 2021:89). In other words, the 'price' for the pandemic and its management will be paid in the long term. And the price will be paid in different areas. The media presented and discussed stories about what came to be known as 'post-COVID' and 'long COVID', that is, health conditions that are a direct consequence of the virus even after the infection has passed. However, the term 'long-term COVID', used to describe symptoms such as fatigue, weakness or difficulties with memory and concentration, was not recognized by Sweden's central platform for information and services relating to health and care, 1177.se. Instead, they followed the recommendation of the National Board of Health and Welfare and used the collective term 'post-COVID'. The indirect consequences of the pandemic were also discussed. The Corona Commission's report shows that social isolation had created extensive and varied problems for many people and their lives:

> As with illness and deaths resulting from COVID-19, the pandemic has also had an uneven impact in terms of the indirect consequences for people's well-being, living conditions, etc. It is clear that already exposed and vulnerable groups have been hit harder than others and that socio-economic and medical factors are of great importance. What has also become clear in a major social crisis like this is the important role of civil society for people. For some people, civil society support has been crucial during the pandemic. The expertise and experience of civil society must therefore be better utilized in the next crisis. (SOU, 2021:89, p 735–36)

The commission's report described the elderly, people with disabilities, people with addiction and people in difficult and violent intimate relationships, such as those subjected to honour-related oppression, as groups that were severely affected but received significant help from civil society. For some people, digitalization helped relieve their isolation, but for many others, technology increased their exclusion. As the commission put it: 'The social debt is also likely to prove unequally distributed' (SOU 2021:89, p 736). Mental health problems that could be attributed to measures taken during the pandemic were a prominent theme in the media during this final period. In an early study from August 2020 on mental illness and the pandemic's indirect consequences, the Public Health Agency came to this conclusion:

> The results continue to point to unchanged or reduced mental well-being and an increase in mental health problems during the initial phase of the pandemic, compared to before the pandemic. The effects are generally small. The results are based on studies from Europe and North America, and one study has been conducted in Sweden. However, most studies do not include analyses of groups at particular risk of mental illness. (Public Health Agency, 2020c)[1]

Just over a year later – in April 2021 – the Public Health Agency published a new report on how public health had been affected throughout 2020. The report found that many people continued to feel good but also that an increasing number of people – especially the socio-economically vulnerable – felt worse:

> Groups that were already living in conditions that put them at increased risk of illness seem to have had a harder time during the pandemic. More people have needed help with housing and food, and for the group of new arrivals, asylum seekers and unauthorized migrants, it has become more difficult to get and keep jobs. It has also become more difficult for certain groups to come into contact with healthcare and authorities, partly due to increased digitalisation. In addition, the isolation and closure of organisations have affected groups with already weak networks and a strong need for support and safe spaces. (Public Health Agency, 2021)[2]

The media and other stakeholders pointed to an increase in mental health problems not only in socially disadvantaged groups but also in other groups, such as healthcare professionals. Torkelsson (2021) reported in *Läkartidningen* – the medical journal published by the Swedish Doctors' Association – that one in three healthcare workers in the county of Östergötland in eastern Sweden was at risk of stress and anxiety problems; by the autumn of 2021, 10 per cent were already showing symptoms of mental illness similar to those affecting people who have experienced traumatic events. Another group that received attention was young people. The issue of their mental health was controversial, as neither researchers nor politicians agreed on the situation. Some argued that young people were more depressed than usual due to social isolation, while others argued there was no evidence of deteriorating mental health in young people.

A study by researchers at the Institute for Futures Studies in Stockholm found that young people in Germany initially felt better at the beginning of the pandemic because 'they needed a break' from their demanding and often hectic lives (Plenty et al, 2021). However, the researchers emphasized that these findings were based on studies at the beginning of the pandemic, and that they did not know how mental health evolved throughout the pandemic. While pandemic-related illness was publicly discussed, our interviewees' stories were characterized by a clear experience of the cyclical and stressful nature of the pandemic. Everything was new in the spring of 2020; as the summer of 2020 passed, people began to believe the pandemic was over, but then everything started again.

Waves in the pandemic: easy and difficult practices

Our interviewees pointed out that both the spread of infection and the organization of work in relation to the pandemic went in waves in the final phase. As one administrative assistant in South Central put it:

> Initially, it was decided that everyone would try to work from home as much as possible in spring 2020. Then the pandemic subsided during

> the summer and most people were back at work again. So, things went smoothly. Then, there was a peak again at the end of 2020. Then, we ended up in the same situation that continued into 2021. Suddenly, in September 2021, everyone was back at work – okay! And then it didn't take so many weeks until – well, then we were home again. (D9, administrative assistant, South Central)

The experience of the different waves of the pandemic explains why this administrative assistant in South Central was no longer surprised by the suspension and resumption of measures and the variation of working conditions: remote and on site. On the contrary, the cycle of work organization became a kind of routine, resembling the unpredictable seasonal weather. The cyclical nature of the changes also meant trying out different ways of organizing. Some people actually felt that certain tasks evolved for the better while they were working remotely and online (see also Chapter 11). During the final period, operations became hybrid in nature, and in several workplaces citizens/customers and employees were allowed to choose how they wanted to communicate with each other and how they wanted to meet. For example, in many schools, all contacts with parents during the pandemic took place over the telephone, but in the spring of 2022, thing were different:

> So this spring, we have said that the parents can choose. The idea was that we would have physical conversations, but we wrote directly that we have had telephone conversations all the time. Let us know if you want to talk face-to-face. If you don't hear from us, we expect you to want phone calls. It has been perfect, and hardly anyone wants it to be different ... I have a few parents in my class who want to come to the school, but these are mainly parents of students who have recently moved to our school who do not really have this established contact in the same way. Most parents continue on the phone because they think it's more practical. (D1, teacher, Central)

The same applied to the introduction of new employees at government agencies and in the organizations of the various municipalities. Starting as a new employee was difficult when everything had to be done remotely:

> I have framework agreements with both the Royal Dramatic Theatre and the Vasa Museum (that is, in my professional groups we are hourly employees). The Royal Dramatic Theatre closed first and then about 20 of us audience hosts received an email saying that unfortunately we would not be allowed to work in the future. At the Vasa Museum, about 25 new employees just had time to sign their contracts before being told that the rest of the training we were supposed to attend in

the spring has been cancelled and that everything is uncertain. (B4, researcher and temporary cultural worker, Central)

On the other hand, when it came to tasks and relationships that were not new, many people felt that the remote working and online communication brought about by the pandemic was an advantage. Even more so, many liked the flexibility and voluntary nature of working practices that became common during the final period of the pandemic, such as the possibility of either meeting people in person or having an online meeting, but also of combining the two:

> I only had corona a few weeks ago, but now I don't think about it at all. I met four people yesterday: it was no longer an issue. We still kept our distance and so on, but in the time before that I was very careful, and when I have tried all other ways, when I have talked on the phone, sent emails and letters, ... then I had finally met people even in real life. But last week I invited people to a Teams meeting instead, and that worked well too. That had never happened before. Certainly not, it was: 'Come to the office at 8:30.' (D2, administrator, children and education, South Central)

This had never happened before, and many people liked the new way of working. They also learnt to work independently in many ways, as contact with other staff was seen as central to the work:

> [I]t used to be easier to go and ask colleagues if you had any questions. Then you just popped your head in to your neighbour and asked them. It was different when we were suddenly at home. You had to find the answers yourself. ... They said 'but you can't just call to ask that'. You felt that asking was a bigger step. Now you've gotten used to it, it's easier to take it on Teams and call someone than it is for me to run and find someone. (D8, economist, South Central)

Digital communication and work also involved the introduction of many information systems. Teams, Zoom, Messenger and Skype were the most common – both for sharing files and for chatting with colleagues, although of course the telephone remained as a work tool. The multiplicity of systems also meant that a new type of work was required to coordinate these systems and their 'pinging'. They were not yet synchronized, and so employees needed to filter different messages. The same administrator in South Central told us:

> You are much, much more available. In the beginning things were ringing all over the place, and the phone was ringing on Teams at

> the same time as the phone, and emails were coming in at the same time as in some other chat group that you were also going to test. None of these systems were synchronized. And then they'd call from reception and say 'there's someone here to see you'. Yes, so if I have to talk in 400 places, I have to ... I think we've all learnt to use the channels, but they still don't work well. Which is really strange, that in 2022 you can't get the system to sync more, like, why doesn't Teams recognize that I'm talking on the phone? (D2, administrator, children and education, South Central)

The expanded, or even new, digital work was one of several themes that our interviewees reflected on when talking about how their everyday work was affected by the pandemic, what they learnt from their experiences and which of the many changes brought about by COVID-19 would fade away and which would become permanent. We return to these considerations in the following chapters.

7

Making Magic

In the words of one of our interviewees, many people were pulling rabbits out of hats to keep the welfare services functioning during the pandemic. This actually led to new ways of working, many of them digital. The 'screenification' of working life became more intense, not only in the performance of tasks but also in social relations and rituals.

When zooming came to villages

One of the most noticeable changes was that meetings were run digitally, via Zoom, Teams or Google Meets. Many IT departments had previously struggled to implement these meeting platforms; now they become familiar to most public sector employees. As one administration manager in North municipality put it:

> I think of all the digital solutions that helped us discover how good it is to have meetings remotely. It doesn't matter if I'm sitting in the building with a colleague or, like now, sitting at the computer and looking at the screen. Even when you live in Northern Sweden you can participate in conferences organized in other places. We hope that this possibility remains, that it does not disappear, that we won't go back to travelling. Digital meetings can also be very good in terms of structuring: I can see sometimes how somebody gets their act together, how they think through what they want to say. We are also much more efficient. There are many advantages, although of course there are some disadvantages as well. (C5, administrator, North)

Many people appreciated digital meetings for their efficiency and because they saved both time and money. Travelling time was reduced, some trips to conferences or training sessions were not needed at all and the time spent waiting for a meeting to start disappeared as people could push the Teams button when they knew it was the right time. The efficiency benefits were particularly pronounced among those who lived far from major cities:

> Now you can attend an eight-hour conference that takes place in Uppsala or Stockholm or Gothenburg, and it's the eight hours that cost you. You sit at the computer and see everything. But if I were to go, it would cost an awful lot of money, and it would require up to two and a half days. (D16, head of administration, South Central)

Reduced travelling time not only meant savings in time and money but also the capacity to attend multiple training meetings or conferences. An environment manager in North told us that 'we can go to 120 training sessions per year, and they don't take as much time' (C6). Meetings could also be recorded and followed up later. Some of our interviewees described it in a way reminiscent of the shift from regular television programmes to streaming and on-demand services:

> Increased efficiency due to reduced travelling time between meetings and the office was also appreciated by those remaining in the office. It was possible to reach people directly through Teams or Zoom, as we used to do by phone, but the new way felt better. As one youth worker said: '[I] make a call on Teams. Because, sure, you can call, but it's not the same.' (D16, head of administration, South Central)

Several of our interviewees told us that their organizations started using new technical systems during the pandemic. South Central was one of the municipalities that introduced a new financial system, and various administrators told us they were able to 'sit and work together without having to move around, so I think we have learnt a lot from this' (D6, technical director). An economist from the same municipality said that 'you could also learn things digitally' (D8, economist, South Central). This applied not only within their own municipality but also across municipal and regional boundaries, for example when municipalities needed to collaborate on issues of procurement, transport, staffing or support for pupils commuting to schools in neighbouring municipalities.

Even if there was less travelling and digital meetings became more accessible, many people found that digitalization had a silencing effect on them. Digital meetings were more efficient, but they also became one-way. One primary school teacher in West municipality said she often avoided talking during Zoom or Team meetings: 'I, who am normally very talkative, was completely silent' (C16, primary school teacher, West). It was more difficult to read clues in social contexts: 'I don't understand when it's appropriate for me to talk. I find those discussions boring ... I hope we can go back to the physical meetings' (C16, primary school teacher, West).

It turned out that efficiency was not the only result of digital meetings. For many interviewees, digitalization meant a change in relationships with colleagues – in several directions. For some, contacts with colleagues, customers and users became much easier thanks to digitalization. A library coordinator in West told us that the implementation of a new technical system made it easier for staff to stay together during the pandemic. They updated each other every week about COVID developments and had better contact with each other: '[W]e are more like a team that will solve this' (C10, library coordinator, West). The pandemic reinforced membership of some working groups and facilitated other processes, such as the introduction of new technologies or adaptations to new ways of working.

People who usually worked alone on certain tasks also discovered that digital meetings gave them new contacts across work groups and organizations. This was the case with an administrator in South Central who worked on education issues. She said she had previously been quite lonely in her little 'childcare bubble':

> I have phoned the principals, who are the ones I serve, but I have hardly ever seen them before, and a phone call is not the same as a Zoom meeting ... So suddenly I got much closer to all those I worked with, and didn't feel as lonely, because I saw the people I worked with, all the time. Instead of sitting alone here in my office, I had lots of new colleagues that I didn't even know I had in the first place, as they had been behind an email, or behind a phone call. And everything became easier to work with, because we could call several people at the same time: instead of three calls, there was one and then we could make a decision. (D2, administrator, children and education, South Central)

It helped that she could see the faces of the colleagues and collaborators she worked with. Other people who also worked across organizational boundaries – with various authorities and with citizens – also found that zooming worked very well, as meetings became 'more efficient, faster' (C1, social secretary, North), and it was possible to arrange tripartite meetings:

> But for others, the transition to digital work meant a deterioration in contacts with colleagues, and, in some cases, almost complete isolation. Many public sector meeting rooms were closed or restructured to ensure the necessary social distancing. Coffee rooms and offices ceased being places for mingling and socializing, to avoid work meetings becoming sources of possible contagion. A business developer in West municipality explained that they had a communal coffee room, 'so there's a big group of my colleagues that I haven't had coffee with for

> a year and it's devastating ... The corridors were silent; an important glue disappeared.' (C15, business developer, West)

The impact on working life was followed by changes in personal life, so feelings were mixed, to say the least. An economist in South Central expressed it as follows:

> [I]t's nice to slow down a bit, it's nice not to have activities seven days a week. But you still miss meeting people ... you're not as sociable as you used to be. Even leisure activities are not the same as before. You haven't socialized with people because you've stayed in your little bubble. (D8, economist, South Central)

At home is good, so why go to the office?

For many people, digital working meant doing their job from home. Reactions to the new – and in many cases enforced – working conditions varied. There were at least four reactions: (1) those who preferred to work at home, (2) those who preferred to remain in the office, (3) those who did not like working at home but got used to it and (4) those who liked having their office at home at first but then found it stressful or boring. Some shifted their attitude towards working from home from being sceptical and negative to learning to appreciate the freedom offered by digital work. Others moved in the opposite direction, especially in the later stages of the pandemic. Long-distance commuters seem to have appreciated it much more: 'Many [colleagues] have actually blossomed ... at any rate, become more efficient. We have many long-distance commuters here, and their work situation has become much better. For them it has been an advantage. I myself live five minutes away, so it doesn't matter to me' (C14, building inspector, West).

Working from home created different challenges from commuting. The presence and interaction with family became more intense, and many people found this lack of separation between work and family life challenging: 'Everyone needs time off from their family sometimes. My job is my breathing space' (C14, building inspector, West). Digital meetings did not act as a breathing space but demanded energy, creating challenges outside of work-related contexts. The smooth transition between family life and work meetings, between kitchen work and office work over kitchen tables was perceived at first as challenging, and after a while as contributing to some apathy and boredom. An administrator told us about her attempts to find the right place for her work at home:

> It was great at first. Loads of freedom, you can do the washing at lunchtime or you can rake leaves in your coffee break or you can

> cook. Great! Much less stressful. That was the first year. ... Then there's a phase where it's still nice but it starts to get a bit, like, boring, so I started moving my office around. It was in the kitchen, then it was in the TV room, then in the bedroom, but then it was getting a bit uncomfortable having these screens and these chairs in my home. And even though I have a lot of contact with both my colleagues and people we work for on a daily basis, I'm still in my house 22 hours a day. I wake up, I do the school run, and then I come back, and then ... I pick them up and then I come back. Because you don't do anything else. (D2, administrator, children and education, South Central)

For some people, things were worse, but others felt that their working conditions improved. An art teacher (B16) in West South went from 'hating' to 'loving' working at home. Similar thoughts were expressed by a training manager in West: 'Of course you long to return to certain things, but many people realize that they have managed to combine work and family life in another way. When they have a child who is ill, they can work from home. And then both the employer and the family are satisfied' (C11, training manager, West).

Again, it is not surprising that reactions change over time. It must be remembered that most people initially thought the pandemic would soon be over. People perceive changes that are expected to be temporary, which can be slightly irritating or even quite amusing, differently from those that are here to stay, which are taken seriously.

Many emotional expressions, often mixed feelings

The pandemic magic evoked a wide range of emotions. Our interviewees tended to use positive emotional expressions when they talked about responsibility and caring, while the negative expressions mainly concerned situations where fear, anxiety, uncertainty and exhaustion were dominant. Most typically, however, negative and positive feelings were mixed.

Responsibility was commented on in different ways and illustrated with different examples, partly depending on the profession the person represented. The seriousness of the situation was obvious in many stories. Some were able to deal with their emotions distantly, within the framework of their professional mission. For others – especially those who had daily contact with students, patients, job seekers or refugees, among many others – the sense of responsibility often became very personal and intense. At home, some found it difficult to let go of thoughts of work, which could lead to anxiety and difficulty sleeping; others felt inadequate, and many experienced feelings of guilt that they had not been hurt by the pandemic as much as those who were less fortunate (especially those working in healthcare). One politician we spoke to was struck by this:

> [T]he stories of protective equipment, of developing skin problems, or of hours of helplessness behind a fogging visor … of grief in the voices of people isolated involuntarily, sometimes couples who've been together for 60 years who have not seen each other for many weeks. After such conversations, I understood that my situation is still more or less normal. (B18, politician, Central)

The media, and personal stories from places and areas where the effects of the pandemic were most severe – healthcare, elderly care, schools – often affected public servants who 'worked in the shadow' of these places and areas. Many of them developed a lingering sense of responsibility that could not be delegated:

> I have worked as a care assistant in elderly care for several years and this is a different kind of stress. You are physically and mentally tired when you go home, but when you go home, someone else has taken over the responsibility. This is not the case now; you're left with decisions and judgements. The responsibility does not end just because you go home. You still have to be there for this person for whom you have decided something. So the responsibility is much greater when you work from home. It's a completely different type of burnout or fatigue from what I've felt before when I've been exhausted or tired. (D12, social worker, South Central)

In the wake of the pandemic, there was also a deep concern among those we met and interviewed in our study: concern for their co-workers, for students, but also for their loved ones. This concern often went beyond the formal role of welfare workers and sometimes included personal concerns, which usually arose when public employees met citizens in different contexts and cases. One teacher told us about a family that he was particularly concerned about: 'The mother belongs to a risk group, they are both a bit older and have some other problems; they have a son who is not always easy to deal with ... I have helped them' (B23, teacher, Central East).

The pandemic has shown that the performance of the welfare state enabled citizens and administrators to develop relationships that went beyond the formal and impersonal. In other words, it was possible to relax the generally bureaucratic and formal way of working that authorities and municipalities usually apply in their work and combine it with more situational and personalized treatment and handling of sensitive cases. The break with working methods, routines, norms and values that are typical of most public sector organizations also applied to situations that were clearly outside their own area of responsibility. A library coordinator described this as follows: 'Much of my concern also centred on the idea of what would happen if I died from the coronavirus: "I wonder if my children will be safe with my cousin and his wife if I die. On Monday, I will get tested at the mobile testing station"' (B18, politician, Central).

Another feeling that significantly affected public employees was fear. This was especially associated with becoming infected at meetings with colleagues and with users and beneficiaries of municipal and state welfare services. A lack of protective equipment intensified this fear, especially in areas where the infection spread the most, such as in elderly care, where staff testified both to their own fears and to the concerns expressed by relatives and visitors. In other areas, such as schools, fear led to unusual attention to signs of infection and discipline around measures such as distancing or hand washing. One teacher in West South spoke of an 'otherworldly atmosphere' throughout the preschool:

> There was something serious and some kind of anxiety in the air and it was difficult to relax, even though in theory we had a very quiet day. You had to think all the time – was someone coughing, have I heard that before today? One child was picking their nose, I had to wash their hands! I accidentally touched my face, when was the last time I washed my hands? It was hand wash and hand sanitiser non-stop. (B6, teacher, West South)

The sense of responsibility, concern, care, fear and anxiety pushed many public sector workers to the limit – not least because the pandemic created more, often completely new, work tasks that they had not yet learnt to handle. Many found it difficult to set limits based on how they felt and strongly testified to their commitment to the 'mission'. This commitment frequently outweighed their own well-being, which often led to a feeling of exhaustion: 'Blast. I wake up at 8 am and turn off the alarm on my mobile phone. I don't know how many times I hit the snooze button. I feel exhausted' (B14, university lecturer, Central).

This feeling of exhaustion seemed to intensify over time:

> I notice a tendency towards exhaustion among colleagues. 'How long is it going to last?', 'I find it so hard to find a good place to work at home', 'I need to meet people', 'Zoom meetings are quite hard work, they are too intense' – from previous comments like 'Why can't we work from home?' (C15, university administrator, Central East)

It was important to set limits but also difficult to do so. It required discipline and the realization that it is impossible to be everywhere at the same time, and that it is also possible to say no. The constant connectivity and availability to answer questions at all times was too much for many of our interviewees: during the first summer of the pandemic, many had to set strict limits during the holiday period and cut all contact with work. One project manager in the healthcare sector told us that there had been too many decisions to be made in just a few months in the spring of 2020, so she decided to be clear before the summer and say to her employees: 'Listen, I don't want you to contact me during my holiday. You have to solve any problems as best you can and if you can't fix something because it's an HR thing, I'll deal with it when I get back' (B25, healthcare project manager, Central East).

Many people, including teachers and administrative staff in local government organizations, complained about the new type of fatigue. Increased intensity of work tasks, uncertainty and unpredictability around their implementation, emotional stress, discomfort and even concerns about unhealthy working conditions were not only associated with experiences from other sectors and other countries (see for example a study from Australia: Lee, 2021). They were also seen by people in our study as part of the new pandemic work that characterized the Swedish public sector.

Most of the emotions described in our material revealed a high level of personal commitment in the welfare work our interviewees were performing. This commitment included both their concern for the citizens and colleagues they worked with, and concerns about their own health and future. Public sector workers did their best to reassure others, rationally informing them about the pandemic and the best measures to deal with it, but they themselves could have nightmares about the personal consequences of a wrong action or judgement:

> Had a bit of trouble breathing, talked to a colleague, checked ... Difficult to sleep last night, such anxiety about the risk assessment … I probably went off and wrote a line or two without thinking – accustomed as I am to letting inspiration, when it appears, take hold ... Despite all the support from the union, I feel lonely and vulnerable. I keep seeing the image of me digging my own grave, the dilemma of the shop steward, is there a difference between the cause and the person? (B19, museum line manager, West South)

Others showed personal vulnerability in relation to their own well-being, which distinguished the pandemic from other 'far away disasters', where you could show compassion without risking your own body:

> Now, however, I had started to worry about my own health ... When I read through various safety guidelines from the authorities, I could only see major risks in connection with certain work activities ... when we cannot keep a safe physical distance from a person who may

> be infected. For example, we may need to take care of or relocate a small child who is sick and then need to carry the child who may be coughing up ... I have worked with the Estonia disaster and the tsunami. The difference was that there was no risk to my own health. (B8, art teacher, West South)

This chapter has illustrated different aspects of what the *magic making* could look like in different parts of the public sector. We have presented a general picture, based on the accounts of people in some 30 different occupations and professions in Sweden's authorities and municipal welfare organizations. In the next part of the book, we describe experiences from three specific sectors: schools, libraries and courts.

8

School: A Profession with Multiple Responsibilities

Writing about how the pandemic has affected teachers and their workplaces cannot be done in a single chapter. As is already known from other reports and publications, the experiences and lessons learnt in Swedish schools are both extensive and complex (Nilsberth et al, 2021; Öckert, 2021). As well as having to expand and adapt their tasks to circumstances they had never experienced before, teachers' and school leaders' responsibilities and workloads grew beyond the ordinary, and they had to rapidly develop new skills and knowledge, not least in digital pedagogy. The new working conditions had an impact on their well-being, and their professional role was redefined in relation to the demands the pandemic placed on schools, pupils and education in general (Lidegran, Hultqvist, Bertilsson and Börjesson, 2021; Lind, Bylund and Stenliden, 2021).

In order to complement the existing knowledge of teachers' responsibilities and work situation, this chapter introduces stories that have a direct link to the discussion on the organization and governance of publicly funded welfare services during the pandemic. The examples used here are taken directly from the accounts of ten teachers, three principals, a head of administration, a youth worker, a preschool teacher and two child and youth workers. In particular, we highlight the conditions under which teachers had to redefine their roles and their professional and human responsibilities. We present some of the lessons teachers say they have learnt from their experiences and some of the – sometimes unique and unorthodox – solutions they have had to invent or adapt to. The chapter concludes with teachers' reflections on what they see as the consequences and future challenges that have emerged in the wake of the pandemic.

As we have already mentioned, we seek to minimize the risk of over-interpretation of the observations in our material. Instead, we want our interviewees to speak in their own voices as much as possible.

The new classroom – stress, sanitizer and uncertainty

When the pandemic became a tangible reality in schools, and not just a distant and abstract danger that was mostly reported in the media, teachers had to be able to quickly settle into their new working environment. How would teachers prepare and organize both classrooms and canteen queues to ensure physical distancing according to the formal recommendations? How do teachers get the youngest students to understand the importance of washing their hands? How do teachers get parents to pick up and drop off their children at school without using the cloakroom and instead convince them to wait outside – even when the thermometer reads below zero? In many cases, the questions and challenges piled up faster than municipality management and school boards were able to come up with relevant and useful advice and instructions. For teachers, the early days of the pandemic were a lesson in both ingenuity and the ability to make decisions based on judgement rather than clear guidelines or recommendations:

Interviewer: You said that you teachers had to improvise. How has the cooperation with the municipality and school management worked?

Teacher: I don't think it has been very good. But it was up to the teachers at the school to solve the problems. And regarding information about the spread of infection in the school. We had to create a messenger group so that we could spread information quickly among ourselves. (C22, home economics teacher, West)

Our evidence is rich in examples of how the ability of individual teachers to find and implement solutions to problems that arose in and out of the classroom appears to be central to their ability to continue teaching, and to provide the care they felt pupils and parents needed:

> I am certainly not one of those people who are in favour of closing schools. I would rather try to make it as good as possible at school and do the best we can. Using the spray, cleaning, talking to them [pupils] and keeping them at home at the slightest symptom. Because closing [the school] would be far worse. (C16, teacher, West)

Having to suddenly come up with new ways of delivering lessons, redefining rules for pupils' behaviour during breaks, improvising new ways of keeping children's hands clean and away from their own noses and each other's faces was an experience that was hard to compare with anything they had experienced before:

> There was a lot of nagging, mainly because the pupils did not take this seriously. They continued as usual. We separated them in the classroom, but then they sat on each other's laps in the corridor. I know that in some schools they stood in the doorway to the classroom with the hand sanitizer bottle and the pupils had to use it. I tried that too, but it fell away pretty quickly. (C17, teacher, West)

At the same time, stories from the teachers show evidence of strong collective support. Many of the solutions and measures introduced by schools at the beginning of the pandemic were based on discussions among teachers and relied on teachers supporting each other: 'I'd say it was a question of different information in similar situations. But then they [school administration] are governed by guidelines from the municipality and the management group there. It's more colleagues and other staff at the school [who provide support]' (C13, teacher, West).

But teachers also looked outside their workplaces for support, tips and feedback on the solutions and adjustments they made. Family members and friends provided emotional support when the work and work environment became too strenuous and exhausting. In some cases, conversations with outsiders provided a reality check – especially when a teacher began to doubt their ability to judge how absurd the working conditions had become:

> At some point I told my friends in Spain about the situation and they couldn't understand anything. So, they really couldn't believe that it [situation in Sweden] was the way I described it to them. At some point I also took pictures in the staff canteen [to show] what it actually looked like. (D17, teacher, South East)

However, during the first months, it became clear that some solutions, innovations and measures needed to be re-evaluated, while others were best abandoned. Not infrequently, teachers explained that they had to make adjustments based on decisions made by school management teams that were often acting under stress and without considering the consequences. In such situations, a teacher might feel that they did not always have enough knowledge or experience to get it right from the start. In other cases, teachers might feel unsure about their ability to question the measures that came from their own school management or from outside, even if they suspected that the measures being implemented were not the best:

> [N]ow [when the pandemic hit the municipality] we would thin out the canteen. Because the pupils were not allowed to take food themselves. They wouldn't touch the ladles, so we had to stand there and serve. ... Then I put my foot down because I just felt that we were

> running around, but for what? We got the children down to their seats, we helped them. Then when I finally got to my seat, the first child wanted more food ... Then when they had finished, I had only eaten half of mine. Then they stand and crowd together in a queue anyway. So, when the next term started, we said that they had to keep their distance in the queue, they are spread out, they have to hold the ladles, then they have to use the spray and then go out. So, there was no congestion when they went out. Many things were probably done with such good intentions that you almost stressed yourself to death. (C16, primary school teacher, West)

The stress, which led to proposals and measures that later turned out to be inappropriate or difficult to sustain, was not only due to the behaviour of school management. Teachers – not least those in the risk groups – could themselves be involved in driving the discussion and actions in what could later be seen as the wrong direction:

> A lot of my colleagues have been very concerned about COVID-19, especially the older colleagues. Those approaching retirement have felt very anxious. And when people have been talking about COVID outbreaks in the neighbourhood, they have been very quick to want to close down their classes and send everyone home. (D1, teacher, Central)

Deviations from the solutions that were put in place at the beginning of the pandemic were also found in the actual teaching contexts. For example, following the 2-metre spacing instructions quickly proved to be something that did not work when dealing with students in the classroom. Due to the difficulties in providing the necessary support to the pupils, the 2-metre recommendation became something that was often ignored:

> I was so surprised when a pupil hugged me. 'What's going on?' We might have become more impersonal during the pandemic, but there are so many other ways to show affection. In terms of helping students, I walk around the classroom the same way I used to. I can't stand 2 metres from the pupil to help in a maths lesson. You have to make the adaptations as best you can. (C13, teacher, West)

But for teachers, managing the old classroom and adapting on-site teaching to the new conditions was only part of the new pandemic working life. Behind dripping hand sanitizer bottles, rearranged classrooms, cluttered staff rooms and chaotic canteens, another transition awaited – one that quickly brought teachers into the digital future.

Teams, distancing and purgatory

For some time now, schools have been talking about the digital transition. Such a transition would involve the introduction of new tools and teaching materials and the development of new pedagogical models and working methods that would take advantage of the potential offered by computers, tablets and online learning platforms – not least in the context of distance learning. What school administrators, teachers and students did not realize was that this development would be given a major boost and that it would challenge the basics of teaching more than they were prepared for:

> It was in April last year [2020], so it was a real challenge right away. I had drilled my students with computers. They have their own computers at school, so there was really no problem. We connected and had distance learning via Teams. So they were the first ones, my class, to have distance learning ... It has worked all the time until now, except for the fact that some choose to sit and play instead. It's distracting, but you can understand that, they're still quite young. It's difficult for the older ones sometimes too. ... not everyone was prepared ... they hadn't tested Teams so it really was baptism by fire. (C17, teacher, West)

Teachers who had not previously worked with digital distance learning had little opportunity to opt out of the digital transition. Lack of the relevant skills or a pedagogical preference for analogue teaching were not valid reasons for not quickly acquiring basic knowledge of how, for example, Teams could be used in classrooms and in meetings with colleagues. In West municipality, the perception that the pandemic had literally thrown teachers and their schools into the digital world seems to be quite common: 'Are there advantages to corona? We have embraced the digital. The teachers who had previously resisted have been thrown into it' (C22, crafts teacher, West).

In other schools and municipalities, the transition to digital distance learning was more complicated. Either they had not progressed far enough in introducing the new tools into their teaching, or both schools and teachers lacked access to the necessary equipment as the demand for computers, cameras and microphones was greater than the rate at which municipalities could procure them:

> Until now we have had rather poor digital resources. We teachers have had our own computers and we have projectors in schools, smartboards in classrooms, but it is only this academic year that all middle school students have their own Chromebook. This is a combined computer and tablet. And in primary school, they work with iPads, but it's not 'one to one', it's half a class set. (D1, teacher, Central)

Due to the technical difficulties and lack of equipment, the transition to digital classrooms was often the most challenging aspect for teachers. How do teachers meet students when the spatial framework changes? How do teachers motivate students who disappear behind black Teams boxes? How can teachers ensure that students have understood their assignments or recognize that they are struggling with the content of the texts?

> But also to try to find equivalent assignments that the children could do at home, where they will benefit from the same knowledge that they would otherwise have received at school. And that is basically impossible. You can't replace that, the discussions and social interaction that you learn at school. You don't get that at home at all. (D1, teacher, Central)

The inability to read body language was seen as really limiting:

> It is precisely that eye contact that you don't have with them [the pupils] that is different. With colleagues we have the cameras on. ... We [teachers] see each other, so it works very well there. But with the students, not everyone is comfortable with it. This particular aspect of distance learning has been both good and less good. (C17, teacher, West)

Limited access to digital tools and equipment and a lack of experience of distance learning were just some of the challenges faced by teachers. Pupils who had limited experience of working with computers, those who did not have access to their own computer at home or those who were unable to participate in distance learning due to limited financial and material resources, mental illness or other family reasons, for example, not only posed practical problems; from the outset, these pupils were less able to cope with the new teaching situation, which also increased the emotional burden on teachers. A common reflection among teachers was that this group of pupils should have been able to continue with place-based schooling. The responsibility for these pupils became even clearer when teaching fully moved to the digital classrooms:

> Because of course we know who they are, we know who these four or five are who can't manage to take that responsibility themselves. To sit at home and listen to lectures and then work digitally and submit digitally. We know who they are. We could summon them to the school. Then we would have a situation where we had teaching at all levels that functioned. (D17, teacher, South Central)

At the same time, there were students who actually felt and performed better when they were able to complete parts of their schooling online. Such students reduced teachers' workloads and allowed them to spend more time engaging with students who needed extra support: 'Those who are usually disturbed in the classroom situation performed much better digitally from home. While those who are [not handling the transition well] can be called in and then we have a manageable number of pupils at the school' (D17, teacher, South Central).

Distance learning and working from home also affected teachers outside their professional context. Organizing a suitable workplace at home was not easy for everyone. Issues with broadband, office furniture and a noise-free working environment became a personal responsibility in the transformation of the home into an office:

> Sitting wedged between a dresser and the bed on a bloody wooden chair and 'talking' about a course with your colleagues on Zoom is so unimaginably far from working together. ... And I realize that this [working from home] is more demanding than I first thought. Having everyone at home, with spatial negotiations every hour about who sits where, who talks the loudest, who has access to a comfortable chair. Or sitting in a café and working – like now. (B8, art teacher, West South)

An unlimited responsibility

Another way to read teachers' stories is to focus on the expanded responsibilities they described as one of the major changes the pandemic brought to their work. This responsibility related in particular to the new skills that were required in relation to students, parents and colleagues in order to adapt teaching to COVID-19. In the case of pupils, it became clear that the primary responsibility for their learning was to be balanced against concern for their physical and mental health. This concern took on new dimensions and began to encompass issues that had previously appeared more in the background and/or concerned only individual students. It ranged from concerns about students not getting enough food when they stayed home from school to how their mental health might be affected when many parents risked losing their jobs due to the restrictions. A teacher in West South articulated her own and her colleagues' concerns in relation to their sense of responsibility:

> I worry about all those who get their only proper meal at school and those with parents who have an addiction and may relapse or get worse when they lose their jobs. Parents with fragile mental health whose health conditions worsened. An awful lot of our students' parents will lose their jobs. (B5, teacher, West South)

Paradoxically, the responsibility for pupils' well-being outside the classroom context might mean that those pupils most in need of support had to be left behind. The lack of qualified teachers, a problem the municipalities had been struggling with long before the pandemic, combined with many teachers being on sick leave, often resulted in a situation where teachers or support staff who would normally be responsible for supporting the most vulnerable pupils were diverted to other activities:

> We were very short of staff at times, but I haven't had to step in and cover for anyone else. But on the other hand, I know that my colleagues who were then in middle school were allowed to do so to a greater extent. Classroom assistants, for example, who are responsible for a specific pupil or pupils who, for various reasons, need to have an adult in their vicinity throughout the school day. The adults were quite quickly taken away from these pupils to cover the pupil groups that were without teachers. There, the children [who needed extra support] suffered. (D1, teacher, Central)

Principals and other people with management responsibilities in the schools and municipalities we interviewed thought along the same lines when they reflected on the extent of the teachers' tasks during the pandemic. In West municipality, the principal pointed out that the teachers' responsibilities had caused their well-being to suffer::

> It was very tough. If you work as a teacher and principal, you have to manage everything. You have to fix everything. It meant that I ended up exhausted. It was a tough workload. So, in the end, it just wasn't possible. It was also tough to realize that I wasn't this superwoman who could do everything. (C8, principal, West)

That the implementation of teaching was, more than ever, dependent on individual teachers' work and their ability to solve problems and challenges both in the classroom and outside became something that teachers themselves perceived as an extended responsibility for their own school's activities and their working environment. This was particularly evident in cases where the teachers perceived contact with and support from the municipality and school management to be insufficient. However, while many teachers took on the extra workload as an extension of their professional commitment and sense of personal responsibility, some of their extended responsibilities also rested on more formal grounds. School boards, municipal administrations and local politicians could be particularly clear in their demands for schools to continue their activities and for teachers to adapt accordingly:

> From the management's perspective, it was taken for granted that the responsibility to keep schools open must be honoured – both at the

> individual and school levels. We discussed the responsibility aspect very quickly as well. No one can back down here; we are responsible for Sweden. … It was clear early on that schools and preschools should be kept open as much as possible. (D15, principal, South Central)

A teacher in West expressed the same line of reasoning when she identified the local politicians and municipal officials as the source of the formal expectations regarding the responsibility that she and her fellow teachers needed to take:

> Politicians, and actually also the municipal officials ... What I could say … they were hiding in the town hall, and the rest of us were expected to work as usual. We got reminders to keep our distance, wash our hands and 'hold out and hang on' and all that. Then we went to work as usual anyway. ... How we felt wasn't important. We weren't supposed to get infected. But I was infected, so I was the black sheep. (C17, teacher, West)

In the ambition to keep the schools open, it soon became clear that 'taking responsibility' could mean different things, and sometimes the opposite of what teachers and school leaders perceived as their main responsibilities during the pandemic. The headteacher in West municipality illustrated the dilemma in the way schools approached responsibility. She described the public pressure for municipalities and school boards to close schools, while teachers and the school boards saw it as their responsibility to keep schools open:

> 'But oh, what do we do now?' Pressure [from the public] to close the school and for us to take our responsibility. But because we had a dialogue with the municipality, the head of the school and the head of infection control, we felt confident that we were doing enough. (C8, principal, West)

The formal responsibility for keeping schools (and Sweden) open and functioning also included the participation of teachers and other school staff in activities and tasks not related to teaching and/or caring for pupils. A head of administration in South Central highlighted the responsibility schools had when his municipality was asked to assist neighbouring municipalities by providing lunches for upper secondary students who could not attend school in those municipalities:

> We have no upper secondary school pupils in our municipality. The vast majority go to Lund or Malmö. We don't have a secondary

> school here. But they [students that attended secondary schools in neighbouring municipalities but lived in South Central] were having distance learning, so we had to make sure that they would get their food boxes. I was also in charge of that. Lunch boxes that they could pick up at our schools here in South Central. (D16, head of administration, South Central)

In summary, the increased responsibilities that teachers took on or were required to manage relied on their commitment and willingness to see their work as much more than just a job. The phrase 'going the extra mile' probably had a different meaning for teachers (as for many other public sector professions) than for politicians:

> I think a lot of it is about not having much choice, and I think teachers are generally pretty good at just getting on with it. Many also feel a lot of responsibility for their students. I think that's one of the biggest reasons why it works. You don't want to let your students down. You fight all the way to the end to make it work for the children. (C18, teacher, Central East)

Thoughts on the future of schools

We conclude this chapter by highlighting some questions about the future that teachers and principals who participated in our study formulated based on the changes and adaptations that occurred in relation to the teaching profession.

Teaching – a profession undergoing reinterpretation

During the pandemic, the teaching profession was reinterpreted in many respects based on the needs and demands placed on teachers and schools. On the one hand, the teaching profession came to be seen as more demanding and more inclusive. Teachers themselves, school managements, municipalities and the general public realized that the teaching profession had a broader scope and more responsibility in the form of more tasks to be handled by and within the teaching profession, and that this increased responsibility placed greater demands on their professional ability to cope with the physical and psychological stresses. On the other hand, the teaching profession became narrower and more superficial as the new responsibilities and tasks displaced some of the activities that teachers themselves saw as central to their professional practice. The areas in which teachers felt that less space was made available were primarily concerned with social contacts with pupils and their parents – contacts which they saw as central, not least in relation to the transmission and shaping of knowledge:

> [I miss] a sensible contact with parents and children in the form of, for example, developmental talks. I really look forward to the open house days that we have jointly with the after-school centre, where parents, relatives and children are invited. An opportunity for an 'off the record' conversation. It doesn't have to be about the child's level of knowledge; you can talk about anything, and suddenly, you have a way into someone you didn't have before. That's the kind of thing I miss and long to get back. (B23, teacher, Central East)

Some of the consequences were seen as positive, and some of the changes and adaptations introduced by teachers and schools during the pandemic seemed to be permanent. Routines that emerged with the shift from physical to digital meetings – both with colleagues and with students – were changes that teachers saw as shaping their profession in the future:

> We have talked a bit at school about what we have learnt during this year – especially what positive things we should take with us. One such thing is, for example, to have short meetings digitally. Because if we are only going to give some information that takes five minutes to convey, then it is better if we do it digitally. Because it saves time for all of us. Another thing that I think has been great is that if you have a progress meeting and a student is sick, you can, if the student is not too sick, have the meeting anyway. (C18, teacher, Central East)

There were changes that teachers hoped would continue after the pandemic; a recurring aspect of these changes concerned autonomy over their work. One teacher in Central expressed a clear desire to retain the responsibility and greater autonomy that working during the pandemic meant for her and her colleagues:

> Responsibility is something you look for. And you want to shape what is included. So I think that in the future I would also really make sure that my colleagues and I make decisions together ... When you say that the school will be closed for a week, I wouldn't take it upon myself to make a plan for all the subjects that I teach – which is three – during this week. But you might decide a little more. That you make a plan [for your] Swedish [class] and you make one for your social sciences class and I make one for my English class. So you distribute the responsibility a little. (D1, teacher, Central)

Pupils

The main concern of teachers in relation to their students and young people more generally was what would happen to the most vulnerable students after the pandemic. The pandemic not only exposed but in many ways also reinforced the vulnerability of socio-economically disadvantaged students, creating future challenges for these students as well as their teachers and schools. How will students from socio-economically disadvantaged backgrounds cope with crises such as COVID-19 when teachers already recognize that these students are struggling?

> I heard that a school somewhere in Sweden was going to map out which secondary school students might need school meals and then allow them to go to a local primary school. Disadvantaged pupils do everything to avoid showing it. Only wealthy and well-educated families are comfortable with receiving help, those who are not afraid of the authorities because they have a safe platform, yes, and those who already have significant help from social services. (B5, teacher, West South)

The lack of social activities such as play, games or sports during the school day was another consequence of pandemic-adapted education. It was not only the activities themselves that were seen as important for students' health; according to the teachers, they were also part of the important socialization process during which pupils shape their future schooling and education. The teacher in the West South school set out his concerns about the students' future:

> I am worried that all these high school kids will have more time to be drawn into the gangs, when their parents are at work and no one is keeping an eye on them. We know that they are recruited as early as 12 years old. There was a 16-year-old who was shot, with ten shots according to his friends. The young people in the neighbourhood are left to their own devices. In the weeks before the shooting, the social workers were out at our school trying to map out what was going on because the criminal environment was brewing. It won't be any less edgy now. (B5, teacher, West South)

However, as mentioned in the introductory sections of this chapter, there were also pupils for whom distance learning and limited social activities had positive consequences in terms of well-being and future prospects (Boström and Rising Holmström, 2023). Some teachers saw opportunities rather than limitations in the expansion of digital elements in education while hoping that these elements would become permanent:

> And it is perhaps [good to have distance learning] for those who have difficulties in larger [social] contexts where there is too much stimulus. And our boys and girls can sit at the computer and play some game for several hours and keep their concentration up and disappear in that bubble. And I can imagine that if they then [in the future] have homeschooling on the screen, it might also be something they can handle better. (D18, youth leader, South East)

When asked about the potential impact of the pandemic on pupils, teachers also cited grade inflation and reduced legal certainty in examinations as risks to their learning and their social well-being. Grade inflation and reduced legal certainty in examinations were cited as examples of risks that teachers linked to digitalization and the more extensive use of distance learning (before ChatGPT and other artificial intelligence solutions were available):

> I worry about when they come back with an even bigger gap to close. How it will affect their ability to graduate in the ninth grade [the final year of Swedish school]. The Swedish National Agency for Education seems to think we can perform some magic when it comes to grading when the students are not there. It can also be difficult to prevent or detect cheating in digital assignments/tests. Here you may need to explore new possibilities to ensure reliability. (B5, teacher, West South)

School and education

Reflecting on post-pandemic school and education, teachers and principals referred to the adaptations and changes they believed would remain after the schools returned to more normal operations. Staffing and competence issues, the digital transition, cooperation with other schools both within and outside their own municipality and the organization of the physical classroom environment were some of the areas where they saw the pandemic as having the greatest impact:

> I think that the way [in which teachers worked during the pandemic] of organizing [teaching] is something we will take with us. How did we solve this when we were short of staff? I think this will also affect how we handle a situation in the schools in the future ... where we do not have enough competent personnel. Where we do not have certified teachers. And then I think we'll end up in situations like this where you might organize things so that one teacher teaches two classes at

> the same time. I actually think you can end up in that situation. (D14, head teacher, East Central)

A teacher in Central made a similar point when she commented on how the school came to limit the use of expensive substitute teachers during the pandemic and instead began to organize teaching to manage with its own teachers. But it was difficult to predict what the way forward – without external substitutes – would look like:

> Perhaps we should think a bit more and evaluate which measures have actually had an effect. ... Of course, there is the matter of substitute teachers. We have some in-house substitutes who work every day and move around. But despite all these substitute agencies and pools, there have not been any who can cover when all the substitutes themselves are sick. ... Thanks to the pandemic, the school has saved so much money on substitute costs because there have been no substitutes to take in. ... But I don't really know how to solve it. Having a higher staff density is always better. (D1, teacher, Central)

Even workplace adaptations that were initially intended to be in place for a limited time seem to follow into the post-pandemic school. How teachers had to adapt classrooms, rest and leisure rooms, canteens and cloakrooms might be an important lesson for the future (Bergdahl and Jalal, 2021). At the same time, the new pandemic-related experiences and insights were easy to misinterpret as they were difficult to sustain in the long run. One of the teachers in South East expressed concern and frustration about which experiences could be used to prepare for and solve future crises:

> At the same time, you see reports in the local press about how brilliant we are at our school because we have a one-way system. And it's great from a pandemic perspective ... only that the principal, on the other hand, does not see that his staff don't give a damn about anything. ... It's just like we're pretending to take it seriously when we're not really doing anything. And then we pat ourselves on the back because we've been so damn good and then we just move on. (D17, teacher, South West)

Teachers and principals also saw that there was much to learn from the lack of communication and dialogue, which in many respects contributed to the perception of school activities as disorganized, difficult to coordinate and with low levels of cooperation – especially between the school and the municipality on the one hand and teachers and parents on the other. One of the common questions related to future school development and preparedness for other crises was how municipalities and schools could be more successful in dialogue and communication:

> Dialogue is very important. You can't have an autocracy, but there must be cooperation and dialogue, both between municipal management and school management, but also with guardians and staff. We are a complex organization. ... It is important that they [teachers, pupils and guardians] know that I am not making things up, but that the entire municipal management is behind it. And vice versa: that the requests I bring to the head of the school and the local government come from staff, pupils and guardians. (C8, principal, West)

Some came to appreciate the way in which the municipalities and school administrations worked with communication, especially the explicit focus on making access to relevant information a 'personal responsibility'. This was something that also appeared in teachers' conceptions of the future school:

> Communication in the municipality has worked very well, although there are always people who feel that they have not received information. It may be the case that it doesn't just come to you but you have to actively look for it. Our platform is Office 365, while the School Department has only used Teams. We were trained in this very early on ... It has been very easy to keep track of, because if someone says that they have not been informed, you refer to Teams. When there are a hundred people on the staff, you can't communicate personally with everyone. (C13, teacher, West)

Teachers felt that better communication would help the schools prepare for future crises, and not least in relation to the role of teachers in shaping this preparedness. Here, the interviewees pointed out that it was mainly teachers who had helped the school find new and sometimes and sometimes demanding solutions to the challenges of the pandemic, solutions that were often outside the formal contexts of the organization of schools and municipalities. But there was also awareness among teachers and principals that the school, the teaching profession and the teachers' work situation often face challenges or crises and that the future organization of teaching/schools will require staff who are adaptable:

> We've had such fantastic staff who have stepped up and covered for each other, so when people have been away, they've taken double classes and triple classes ... But that doesn't mean that people have asked things like 'what do we do now if we end up in this?' but that they knew that this was how things were done here. ... There was a

> breadth of experience [among teachers and principals] that enabled them to deal with the issue even if they did not link it to the pandemic. (D14, principal, South East)

Beyond the educational mission

In this chapter, we have focused on the teachers' and principals' efforts to ensure that teaching could be carried out despite the restrictions and conditions created by the pandemic. It soon proved difficult to fulfil the tasks and responsibilities of primary and lower secondary schools as specified in the Education Act and the Education Ordinance (2010:800), while they also had to be broadened and developed in everyday life. One aspect that is not mentioned here, but which we return to in the final chapter of the book, is the impact of COVID-19 and the pandemic on the democratic mission of schools and teachers: 'Education should be designed in accordance with fundamental democratic values and human rights such as the sanctity of human life, the freedom and integrity of the individual, the equal value of all people, gender equality and solidarity between people' (Swedish Education Act 2010:800).

Although the teachers and principals in our material did not explicitly consider how their work during the pandemic related to the values and rights that form the basis of the democratic mission, it became clear that many of the adaptations made in the schools had a direct impact on issues such as inclusion, equal treatment, discrimination and students' rights and freedoms. Being able to ensure everyone's access to digital education, organizing distance education in a way that did not violate the integrity of pupils and/or their families and being able to enforce school attendance without simultaneously stigmatizing certain groups of students are just some of the issues that have clear links to the school's status as a democratic institution. It also became clear that some decisions taken by school boards and school administrations were anchored purely in the democratic structures and processes of the municipalities. For instance, in the context of issues such as taking on unqualified teachers, limitations on supervision and support and changes in working practices, where teachers' mandates could be extended or limited without prior negotiation with the municipality and labour unions, one might expect the usual democratic processes in which these types of issues should be anchored to have been downplayed or even side-stepped.

9

Librarians, Libraries and Social Mission during the Pandemic

Signe Jernberg

As with the other areas of public sector provision discussed in this book, libraries were badly affected when the pandemic arrived in Sweden in the spring of 2020.. Forced to reduce their opening hours, and in some cases to shut their doors entirely, libraries ceased to be places where people went to read newspapers, print documents, borrow books, participate in seminars and book circles, and to have coffee with old friends or make new ones.. Visitors would be 'in and out' to do their most essential business.

During the pandemic, it was made clear that libraries not only administer book loans but also have a broader mission in society. The Swedish Library Act 2013 states:

> Public libraries shall promote the development of a democratic society by contributing to the dissemination of knowledge and the free formation of opinion. Libraries in the public library system shall promote the status of literature and interest in education, enlightenment, training and research and other cultural activities. Library activities shall be accessible to all. (Library Act 2013:801)

People go to libraries to borrow, read, search and converse. Libraries include a variety of tangible and material objects and activities: rooms, bookshelves, books, circulation desks, children's corners, reading rooms, computers, magazine racks and so on, objects and activities that are rarely questioned in times of stability. This also hides their purpose. When both artefacts and actions are challenged, as during the pandemic, and in a large-scale, pervasive and drastic way, their purpose is also brought to the surface. The pandemic burrowed into the very heart of libraries and highlighted their social mission: to be a pillar of contemporary democracy. The impact of the pandemic on libraries thus provides an opportunity to explore and discuss the position of libraries in Swedish democracy.

This chapter examines how libraries were affected by the pandemic, particularly in relation to their democratic and social mission, as well as how librarians and library assistants worked to adapt their activities so that the requirements of the Library Act could be met. For this purpose, national news reporting on libraries during the pandemic was selected, with a particular focus on descriptions of how libraries succeeded in adapting their activities. This quantitative media material is then supplemented with quotes from the interviews on which this book is based.

Democracy and libraries

Libraries, in line with the Library Act, have long been seen as a pillar of the democratic state, both nationally and internationally (see, for example, Kranich, 2001). The question of libraries as an element of liberal democracy has been particularly topical in recent years in connection with discussions about, for example, the impact of information technology on democracy, knowledge as relative and/or absolute and the questioning of the foundations of democracy through populism and the re-emergence of autocratic states (see, for example, Kranich, 2020; Wikforss and Wikforss, 2021). The issue of libraries and democracy was also raised during the pandemic but on more substantive grounds than in academic discussions: the unique societal role of libraries was highlighted in the wake of reduced opening hours, closures and altered services as a consequence of the spread of the virus (see, for example, Eriksson, 2020; Kjellgren et al, 2020). The question of the library as an accessible or inaccessible place came into focus.

The Swedish Library Act and the subsequent organization of Swedish libraries are part of a tradition of thought in which the definition of democracy and its prerequisites are developed into something more than the original 'will of the people', where power is exercised through the will of citizens. The basic concept of democracy is not sufficient for us to understand and justify the need for libraries. Instead, this chapter uses a definition that includes a variety of elements that ensure people's rights and freedoms, such as freedom of speech and freedom of the press. Monk (2018) argues in favour of separating the concept of democracy from such elements and isolating it to 'a set of binding electoral institutions that effectively translates popular views into public policy', suggesting that the rights and freedoms of individuals are instead included in the term 'liberal'. Thus, a liberal democracy is a democracy that, by definition, has institutions that translate the will of the people into policy and protect freedoms and rights. Sweden can thus be said to be a liberal democracy.

However, this reasoning is still not sufficient to understand why we have libraries and library legislation and how libraries function as a pillar of a liberal democracy. Understanding this needs a deeper concept of democracy that focuses on what is required for people to be able to exercise their rights to participate in democracy. Wikforss and Wikforss (2021) refer to Dahl and his concept of 'enlightened understanding', which implies that people in a democracy need to be given the opportunity to inform themselves about political alternatives and their consequences, as such opportunities do not exist automatically. Rather, the maintenance of democracy involves developing and maintaining channels for information through the public sphere. Dahl's concept of democracy also includes the premise that the state is not only responsible for providing information and opportunities to develop knowledge but also for ensuring that everyone has equal access to it. The Swedish Library Act contains an equality dimension: that libraries should be accessible to all (The Swedish Library Act 2013:801, section 2). This also means that loans of literature should be free of charge (The Swedish Library Act 2013:801, section 9), which speaks directly to Dahl's concept of democracy.

Against the background of this concept, the Swedish Library Act and the library system are understood as pillars of a liberal and egalitarian democracy. Together with, for example, the media – where press subsidies can be said to fulfil a similar function to libraries – libraries are information channels for people to exercise their right to vote, based on an enlightened understanding of society and the political system. Libraries are often constructed in this way, as good institutions with the inherent capacity to promote democracy, with equal access, where citizens use libraries and develop an 'enlightened understanding'. However, the library as an institution has also been challenged by, among others, Popowich (2019), who describes libraries as supporting an apparent and unequal democracy. The development and existence of libraries follows a trajectory from the Age of Enlightenment to today's neo-liberal societies, where liberal democracy is, in fact, unequal and surrounded and penetrated by market forces to a much greater extent than the discourse on both libraries and liberal democracy would have us believe. In this way, libraries become a way of legitimizing an unequal liberal democracy.

Wiegand (2015) puts forward another criticism: that libraries are in fact places people visit, and that the services provided have little to do with libraries as guardians of democracy and co-creators of what Dahl calls 'enlightened understanding'. Libraries do other things. Popowich's and Wiegand's criticisms were made in an American context, but Willstedt (2020) and Engström (2020) have shown that the Swedish library system has the same problems, even if neither author is as strong in their criticism as Popowich, for example. Engström (2020) highlighted, among other things, the national library strategy 'The Treasure Chest of Democracy', which bears strong traces of the idea of libraries as 'good'. Consequently, there is reason not to highlight libraries as being only one of several good things in liberal democracy but also to problematize their design and existence.

Librarianship is a relatively young profession in Sweden. It was only in the 20th century that training and specific skills created a paid profession (Thomas, 2008). Previously, similar tasks were carried out as an unpaid side-line to other professions, often by teachers (Thomas, 2008). Even further back, libraries, in the sense of book collections, belonged to the church and monastic system (Ettarh, 2018). In a research study, the Swedish Library Association (2008) showed that librarianship includes a variety of tasks and professional identities.

In a research overview, the Swedish Library Association (2008) shows that the librarian profession encompasses a multitude of tasks and professional identities and is characterized by professionalization efforts, while the professional competencies remain unclear and are linked to both technological and political societal development. They described the profession as fragmented and difficult to define, yet very clearly tied to a specific place (libraries) and a specific law (the Library Act). Librarians are thus defined by the fact that they work in libraries (Swedish Library Association, 2008). Another way of defining librarianship is through the values that hold the professionals together. Here, the Swedish Library Association highlights research that shows that the profession is characterized by 'certain specific values, namely to ensure free access to information for citizens'. Guaranteeing free access to knowledge is the characteristic that librarians have in common (and is thus more important than, for example, a common and unique knowledge base), which also serves as a connecting link for the entire profession. This formulation speaks directly to both the Library Act and Dahl's concept of democracy. Librarians thus become a link between legislation and an idea and the users of the libraries.

Consequently, part of the libraries' mission is to be accessible to all citizens. The broad access to what libraries have to offer is a prerequisite for libraries to fulfill their mission. Likewise, it is a prerequisite for libraries to be considered a pillar of a liberal democracy, but also for them to be questioned as such, and for them to be utilized by the citizens. Swedish libraries and their activities affect many people in society, some on a daily basis, others more rarely. Prior to the pandemic, in 2019, there were 56,788,303 physical loans from public libraries in Sweden (Ranemo, 2020). The number of active borrowers, meaning those who borrowed at least one book a year from public libraries, was 26 per cent of the population (Ranemo, 2020). In the same year, the average Swede visited a library six times (Ranemo, 2020).

A Novus survey from 2018 (Novus, 2018), commissioned by the Swedish Library Association, investigated library use among the Swedish population, and more than 1,000 interviews were conducted among a randomly selected panel representative of the Swedish population. One question asked was how frequently respondents visited libraries. A total of 54 per cent responded 'at least once a year', which suggests that far more people visit libraries than borrow physical books. Some 82 per cent said they felt positively or very positively about libraries in general. Respondents were also asked to match statements regarding reasons for visiting libraries with their own view of libraries, with 58 per cent answering 'peace and quiet', while 14 per cent answered 'meeting place'. The statistics show that Swedish libraries as institutions are well-frequented places that offer information, reading and book loans and an opportunity to meet other people, as well as peace and quiet.

While libraries are seen as a vital public service that is visited and used by a large part of the population, they are not, however, essential to society on a daily basis. The closure of a school has immediate and far-reaching practical consequences for many parents. A hospital has to operate on a daily basis. If a library closes for a day, nothing obvious happens: no one dies, no one gets sicker, no one is prevented from going to work, no one goes without food, no rubbish is left to pile up. What does happen is that the possibilities of developing 'enlightened understanding' are challenged, which is, of course, a far more abstract consequence than piles of rubbish. Throughout the pandemic, libraries found themselves in a situation where the notion of being a socially important activity, which satisfies long-term, abstract, but not acute needs, not only had to be given meaning but also practised in a completely new world. The libraries found themselves in a situation where their activities needed to be redesigned so that their social mission could be fulfilled.

When the pandemic came to libraries

Let's now look at what happened to libraries and their social mission during the pandemic. How did the media report on why library activities were affected as they were? And who, which professional group or position of responsibility, expressed their views in the articles? This is followed by a more detailed illustration of how the pandemic was handled by delving into how the libraries remained open or closed, and by seeing how their activities were adapted to recommendations and the spread of infection.

Pandemic vs social mission: why are libraries changing their activities?

There were two main themes in media reporting on how changes in library activities were justified, discussed or explained during the pandemic. These related to the spread of infection and the authorities' recommendations on the one hand and the libraries' social mission on the other. Figure 9.1 shows how changes in library activities were motivated, discussed and explained during the pandemic.

The diagram shows that the mission of democracy and society was an issue that emerged almost simultaneously with the first confirmed cases of COVID-19 in Sweden. The discussion of democracy and the social mission of libraries was covered in roughly the same number of articles during the first and second wave, but relative to the total number of articles written about libraries, the discussion of democracy and libraries' social mission was stronger during the first wave. The articles dealing with how changes in library activities were justified, however, focused much more on the spread of infection and the authorities' overall recommendations. It was during the second wave in the autumn of 2020 that pandemic-related justifications became more prevalent. Changes implemented due to staff shortages or because of a desire to protect staff from infection did not follow the same pattern. These explanations had occurred relatively infrequently in the material throughout the period, with a small peak in the issue of staffing at the beginning and end of the pandemic, and a small peak in the issue of staff safety during the second wave.

One obvious conclusion is that the social mission of libraries was actualized and challenged by the pandemic and thus also became part of the media reporting. At the same time, several articles highlighted the spread of infection and the authorities' recommendations. Further on, we see how the spread of infection and recommendations can be understood as linked to the libraries' mission but as a more direct impact on their daily activities.

Managers and different professions in the media

Who was given space when libraries appeared in the media was another interesting aspect. Figure 9.2 shows the number of articles in which different professional groups spoke about the issues facing libraries. In the articles, the voices of library, culture, or leisure managers are most frequently featured, followed by those of librarians.. These groups received more media coverage in the first and second wave, in the spring and autumn of 2020, while general managers had a much higher media presence in the second wave. Other professional categories, and above all other high-ranking officials within the municipality, that is, municipal directors, chairs of municipal boards and chairs of various committees, also had an increased presence during the second wave of the pandemic, albeit to a much lesser extent.

The democratic and social mission was clearly emphasized during the first wave. It was also during this period that librarians received extensive media attention, possibly due to the earlier-mentioned link between the social mission of the libraries and the users of their services. During the second

Figure 9.1: Analysis of media articles discussing changes in library activities during the COVID-19 pandemic

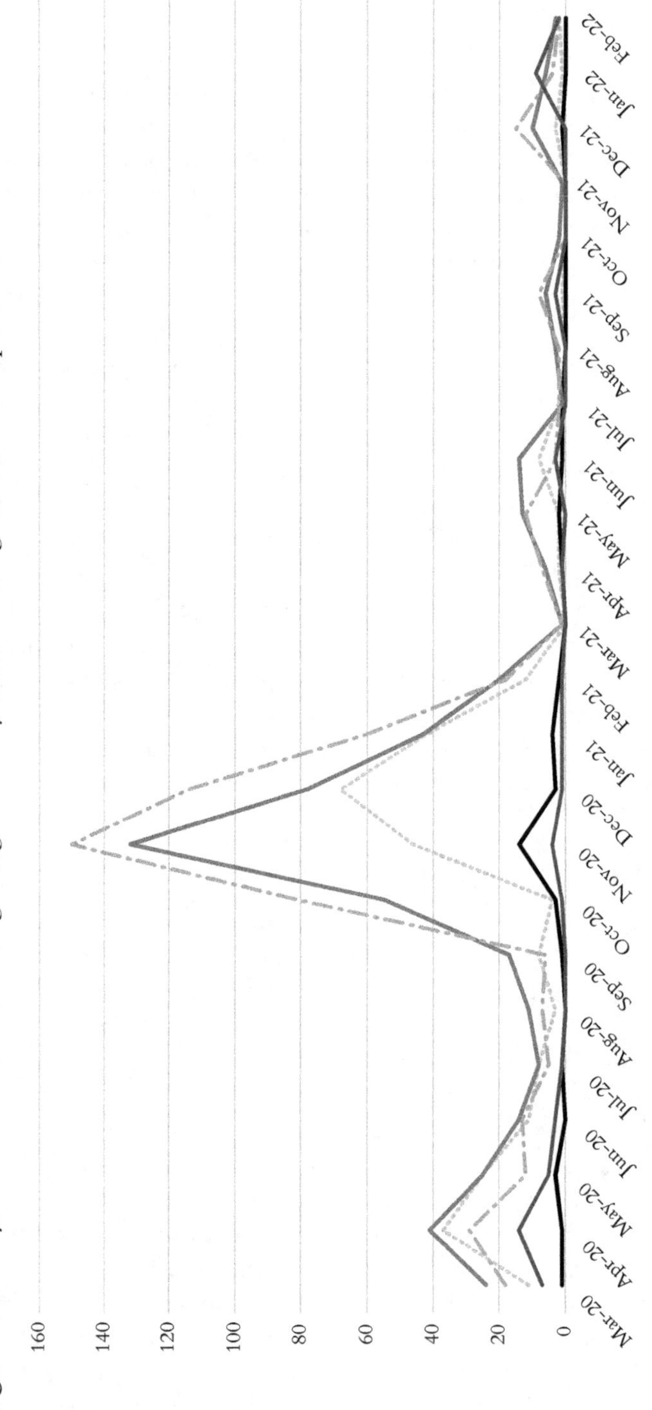

Source: Mediearkivet

Figure 9.2: Occupational groups cited in media articles about libraries during the COVID-19 pandemic

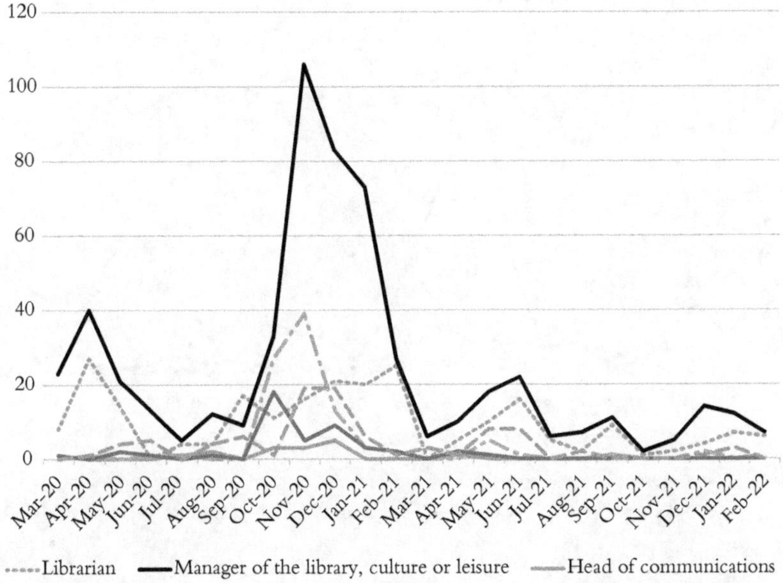

Source: Mediearkivet

wave, the discussion was more about the authorities' recommendations and the spread of infection in general. Then, it was the library directors who were given space. Perhaps, as a link between bureaucracy and libraries, they were forced to talk about infection control rather than missions.

Open – closed

As with so many other organizations, news reporting on libraries came to focus on the question of whether they should be open or closed. Figure 9.3 shows the number of articles mentioning different types of changes in library activities for each month between March 2020 and February 2022. The largest category is the one related to changes in the opening hours of libraries (closing, opening or changing their opening hours). This category grew particularly in October 2020, peaked in November 2020 and then gradually decreased until March 2021. Most of the local advice in November 2021 was to avoid indoor environments such as libraries. But it was only in December that the central government urged municipalities to close libraries completely.

Opening/closing was the most frequent theme in the articles. The perception of whether libraries were open or closed tended towards a duality in the news articles. If a library closed the entrance door, it was perceived as closed,

Figure 9.3: Media articles covering actual changes in library activities during the COVID-19 pandemic

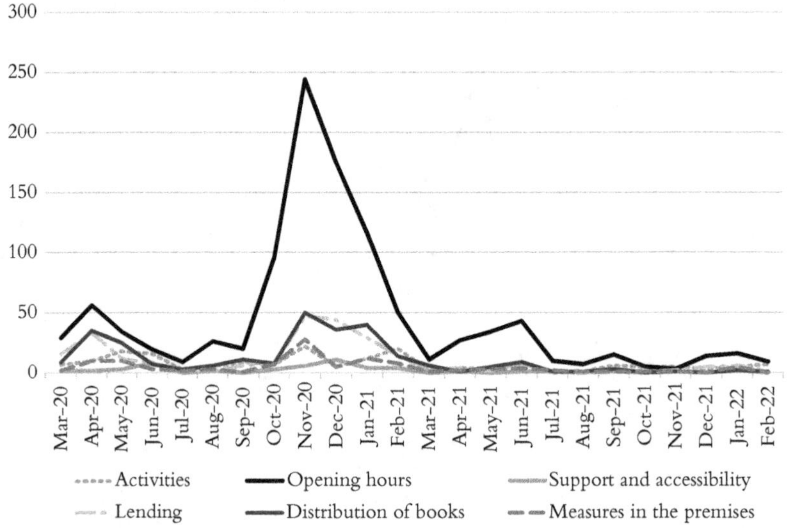

300
250
200
150
100
50
0

Mar-20 Apr-20 May-20 Jun-20 Jul-20 Aug-20 Sep-20 Oct-20 Nov-20 Dec-20 Jan-21 Feb-21 Mar-21 Apr-21 May-21 Jun-21 Jul-21 Aug-21 Sep-21 Oct-21 Nov-21 Dec-21 Jan-22 Feb-22

Activities — Opening hours — Support and accessibility
Lending — Distribution of books — Measures in the premises

Source: Mediearkivet

no matter how many alternative ways there were to access what the library provided, such as collection points, digital story hours and borrowing by phone. If the door was closed, the library was closed. If the door was open, the library was open, if only to go in for 15 minutes, borrow a book and go out again.

Book bags, digital storytelling sessions and collection points – alternative availability

Libraries are not just about book loans; they are physical places that fulfil different functions for different people. They provide a range of activities and opportunities beyond lending. Based on the material we have collected and analysed, it was the libraries' lending activities that were first transformed when the pandemic arrived, and a major focus was on finding different ways to make books available. A few months later, the 'what' question instead began to focus on whether libraries could be accessed and what activities they were able to offer. There seemed to be a need to try to redesign more parts of the organization once the lending issue had been at least partially resolved. Some libraries experimented with digital book circles and outdoor story times. The need for support was recognized, the issue of accessibility became central and the libraries tried to figure out how to support people who were not part of the digital world in accessing the increasingly digitized library.

The second largest category in the analysis of the changes that took place in libraries' operations were those relating to lending – changed lending rules, return through book deposits, increased use of e-media and the like – and physical distribution of books (book bags and home delivery). These changes peaked during the first and second wave of the pandemic but with a slight delay in relation to the 'opening hours' category during the second wave. Indeed, many of these services, such as home delivery, were already in place when the second wave hit. Their reappearance in the material during the second wave may be due to libraries actively reminding people of these services as the restrictions were tightened and certain decisions, such as the cancellation of late fees, were extended.

The least frequent categories concerned measures on the libraries' premises, changes in their activities and changes in support functions and accessibility. The number of articles mentioning measures on the premises rose temporarily at the beginning of the pandemic but peaked in November 2020 and then declined in December of the same year. A review of the articles in November suggests that changes to library premises came in response to the increased spread of infection and the new general recommendations. By physically adapting their premises, libraries tried to make it possible for visitors to use the library while still keeping their distance. Questions related to library support services and accessibility peaked in June, and changes in their activities seemed to be most frequent in May, June and November 2020, as well as in February 2021.

Voices from the libraries

This chapter has so far highlighted the nature of media coverage during the pandemic and the issues that were most frequently reported on. However, the categories were abstract and isolated from each other. To better understand the categories and how they might be related, we now turn our attention to the library staff interviewed in the project on which this book is based, allowing them to play the role of commentators on the quantitative material.

Making libraries accessible during a pandemic

Accessibility is included in the Library Act, and it is clear from the quantitative data that this was jeopardized during the pandemic. Libraries were closed and activities were restricted, not least because certain groups in society were advised to severely limit their presence in public places. One librarian directly related the closures to restrictions on the democratic mission:

> So this meant that much of the library's mission, which is to be accessible to everyone, and our democratic mission to provide information and so

> on, was limited, because people in South Central could not access the library and sit at a computer and look for information. You couldn't read newspapers in our library, you could only reserve books and collect them. And this was a restriction for more than six months. (D3, library coordinator, South Central)

A library assistant expressed similar thoughts: 'These were very practical questions. How and when to close or not to close. As a cultural worker or library worker, you want to be open as much as possible. You want it to be accessible. At the same time, you want to protect both visitors and staff' (D5, library assistant, South Central). At the same time, the librarian gave examples of alternative modes of distribution and activities, which were then transferred to the digital world. When libraries closed, another world opened up. The library coordinator in South Central explained: 'We've had a lot of digital programmes, we've had digital book circles, digital lectures, instead of having crafts for children on site, we've handed out reserved books and craft bags that you could pick up. So we've really tried to adapt, just like other libraries in Sweden' (D3, library coordinator, South Central). He went on to reflect on the physical meetings and the library as an important meeting place: 'The library is still a meeting place where you meet people and even though a lot of our activities have been and will be digital in the future, it is still this meeting with people, the physical meeting, that is important. And I have missed that very much' (D3, library coordinator, South Central).

The profession as a link between the idea of the library, the law and the users

When COVID-19 started to spread beyond China and then Italy, everything happened very quickly. And the changes initiated in the public sector in the first weeks and months were something that characterized almost the entire pandemic. It was a time of trial and error as people found new ways to live their lives, organizing their private and work-related tasks and learning to relate to a society that no longer functioned in the way most people were used to. The library staff we interviewed said that more guidance and advice on procedures would have been helpful:

> Here, you have wished you had some support [from the municipal management]. That they [the managers] go in and say that they [the libraries] are closed this way and this much. They haven't done that, they've let us decide for ourselves. Then my manager made a proposal [for how to close/open the libraries] and they said okay. There have been no discussions about that. There are pros and cons. You want

> some top-down control in serious crises, but we didn't get that. I think they felt insecure about this. (C10, library coordinator, West)

The interpretation of the formal advice and restrictions was left to the libraries and those working there:

> SKR [Swedish Association of Local Authorities and Region] had to look at the legal aspects. Then the CC [chief of infection protection at the municipality] made recommendations in December/January saying that it was okay to close down to a certain extent. And how do you interpret that? We interpreted it as having a book collection point at the back. People could order and pick up books but not enter the library. It is all a question of interpretation. (C10, library coordinator, West)

Another interviewee pointed out that some decisions were based on ignorance of what the library as a physical place looks like, and what the risk of infection was. The librarians wanted to adapt but were not allowed to:

> I think it was completely unreasonable that the libraries were closed. You could have had the library premises open without any risk of spreading infection. Libraries are not a place where infections are spread in general, nor are people crowded here in other contexts. Even if we sometimes have a lot of visitors, it's not like that. (D3, library coordinator, South Central)

Some frustration about both too little control and too much was expressed in the interviews. At the same time, positive aspects also emerged – for example, one interviewee showed how library staff in Sweden worked together to find new ways to make their activities accessible:

> There has been a tremendous amount of creativity in the Swedish libraries, I would say, and we have given each other tips. There is a Facebook group called 'the pandemic library' where people give each other tips and discuss how to handle this situation when we may not have so many visitors or have closed completely. (D3, library coordinator, South Central)

Libraries beyond democracy – and their social mission

The pandemic not only exposed the democratic social mission of libraries; it also made visible things that libraries are used for that are not necessarily part of their core mission. The librarian in South Central told us about people who used the libraries for other purposes, such as looking for accommodation, travel or jobs. The librarian also noted that

> [t]he fact that we have not been able to use a computer or print out a form is something I have found quite unreasonable. We could have let people book a computer, come in, sit for a while, print out and so on, but we weren't allowed to do that. I feel that was a limitation, that they couldn't apply for housing on a computer, they didn't have a computer at home and so on. And we found it very, very difficult to get information about where we could refer them to. (D3, library coordinator, South Central)

A library assistant told us that these sorts of activities increased rather than decreased during the pandemic – when other activities were closed down, the libraries became a kind of public place where people could get help with various private matters:

> I don't know if there was a fear of making the wrong decision, as I said we want to be open as much as possible, we want to be accessible. And then when other societal institutions closed down, we became ... well, opposite our library there were things like banks and institutions like that, and I don't really know what it looked like with everything, but it was noticeable that people came in to us and wanted more help, with official papers and things like that, which they perhaps didn't get. Banking, I mean printing out bank statements and stuff like that, because they couldn't access the bank physically. (D5, library assistant, South Central)

Revisiting libraries and democracy

Libraries are a physical place whose accessibility appears to be essential for everything the library offers. This was obvious 30 years ago, when libraries were dependent on their physical premises and digitalization was in its infancy. Today, the line between where the library is and where it is not is more fluid: large parts of the library are online and almost always open. Given how many people visit libraries without looking to borrow a book, it is not surprising that many news articles were written about their physical accessibility. They were perceived as closed when the door was closed. The library is a place that seems to have an intrinsic value as a place to go for peace and quiet, to meet, to be educated, but also as a place where people can go because they have not mastered the digital solutions that prevailed during the pandemic. When the door to the library was closed, another door was opened – to increasing digital exclusion.

The distribution of books was a constant issue in the media. Libraries are much more than books, but these still seem to be the main items that much of the media coverage focused on. Much of the work of librarians initially focused on developing alternatives to make literature accessible and then continued with other activities. Even during the pandemic, librarians continued to act as a link between the idea of libraries as a foundation of democracy on the one hand and users on the other.

The interview material also shows that in an equal democracy, libraries fulfil a function that goes beyond 'enlightened understanding'. Before the pandemic, the library was a place where people could do private business, such as looking for accommodation or employment or making contact with government authorities. It is difficult to understand this as part of the quest for enlightened understanding: rather, it is about giving computer access to groups who, for various reasons, do not have a computer at home. The librarian who gave this example also seemed to see it as an obvious part of the library's activities in that the library has other tasks and responsibilities in addition to providing information and access to knowledge. The Enlightenment ideal is thus joined by a more political ideal of equality.

When the pandemic hit, it also affected the role of libraries as a place of equality. The pandemic brought the library's democratic and social role to the fore, and the role of the library as a place for the development of 'enlightened understanding' was highlighted through media reporting and through the work of library staff. Although those most affected by the pandemic were those who could not take part in the libraries' new digitalized world, it appears that libraries have become a safe haven for marginalized groups. Libraries as an institution were intended to have a different role but have become something more. Perhaps because no one else did.

10

Courts and the Pandemic – Virtual Trials and Algorithmic (In)justice

Charlotta Kronblad

Imagine this: You are standing outside a magnificent court building in the centre of the city where you live. You have already walked up a couple of steps to the entrance, and in front of you is a massive wooden door. The door feels heavy under your hand, but you resolutely push the handle down and push it open and enter. Your footsteps clatter on the polished marble floor. You feel a little nervous. You got up early and are dressed to appear in court. It doesn't really matter whether you are in court this day as a witness, a plaintiff, a suspect or a party to a civil or family case; whatever your reason for being here, this is a new place for you. You are facing an unusual and important event, and you have prepared and dressed yourself carefully. The very air is full of seriousness, and you can almost smell the professionalism. A few lawyers pass you, well dressed in dark suits, leather briefcases in their hands and a lingering trace of exclusive perfume. Your case is called over the public address system, and you hurry to the right room. As you enter the courtroom, you see the judge in a prominent position right in front of you. Next to the judge is a notary who is taking notes in a loud voice. You think you recognize the setting from a detective film you saw a week ago. The prosecutor, the injured party and the counsel for the injured party are crowded together on one side of the podium, and the defence lawyers and the defendants on the other. You sit down in your designated seat and look around in wonder. It is a professional arena where justice is about to be done, but it also appears to be a theatre full of actors with clear role descriptions, each with their own special props.

Instead, imagine this: You are sitting quietly in your own home. You've combed your hair and put on a nice shirt, but since no one will see your legs, you're wearing the sweatpants you threw on when you got up this morning. The smell of coffee wafting from the kitchen reminds you that a pot is ready, and you refill your cup. You return to the living room, where you take out your computer or smartphone, log in and click on the link sent to you by the court. You enter the court's digital waiting room and are then accepted into the digital courtroom. You are admitted and see the different actors of the court in front of you on the screen. The judge in one box, the prosecutor in another, the lawyer in a third. The trial can begin.

The latter example is a simple representation of what a virtual court is or could be. And virtual courts are something that became a reality during the pandemic. Due to the restrictions imposed worldwide, in many countries it was no longer possible to hold trials on site, which meant that alternative solutions had to be found. The administration of justice cannot be cancelled, as it is necessary for the functioning of society. This meant a major practical change for those who worked in the courts, as well as for other actors who would participate in the trials. In addition, it also meant a significant shift in thinking – a fundamental mind shift. Changing the court from a physical place to a digitized provider of justice implies a clear institutional change. We move from the court as a place to the court as a service, which means significant changes for those who work in the place and for those who are served by the justice service.

In this chapter, I will review what this shift has meant and what it enables going forward. In the next section, I will explain the role of the court in society and describe what the digital transformation means in general, and what it means more specifically for the judicial process. I will then describe the transition to virtual courts during the pandemic in different parts of the world, addressing the risks, advantages and disadvantages of virtual trials. I will also discuss the increasing problem courts face in resolving complex digital legal issues and dealing with complex digital and algorithmic evidence. Finally, I will suggest how the *mind shift* brought about by virtual courts may also help solve these new, and growing, challenges of algorithmic injustice.

The importance of courts as independent institutions supporting democracy

The introduction to this book states that the pandemic has had a major impact on the public sector, and on those who work in it. But it can also be said that, beyond this, the pandemic has had far-reaching consequences for key democratic processes and for the principles and values of society. It is in this light that this chapter should be read. For the judicial system, the pandemic posed a major challenge because a functioning judicial process is a prerequisite for sustaining modern society and for fulfilling its democratic ideals and values (Susskind, 2019). By guaranteeing and upholding *the* law, and operating in accordance with the *rule of* law, our courts create the conditions for legal certainty in society. To fulfil this, an independent judicial system that can deal effectively and fairly with the legal issues it faces is essential. This requires a smooth process where there is a place or arena where disputes can be resolved and justice done, as well as public legitimization of legal practices through trust in the system and continued support for its institutions. The operational legal system is thus invaluable for creating legal and security conditions for both the public and private sectors, and for ensuring that legal certainty, stability and justice are maintained in society (Webley et al, 2019).

Over time, these social institutions have developed specific processes and symbolism that reinforce their values (Siebert, 2020). Justice is manifested in material assets such as thick law books, heavy wooden clubs and shiny silver scales. In Anglo-Saxon countries, items such as hoods and wigs are also used to symbolically demonstrate that the professional actors take on a professional role in their office and that they represent the institution in their professional practice. The courts therefore become theatres that gain legitimacy and public trust through the display of these symbols, and through the maintenance of ceremonial processes and clear institutions (Siebert, 2020). Thus, during the pandemic, these ceremonial and material attributes took a back seat as courts had to quickly adapt to the new reality. And in the digital world, there is no obvious place for material symbols.

In addition, the physical restrictions and behavioural rules during the pandemic meant that additional challenges arose in the administration of justice. While it was of the utmost importance that processes could continue and trials be held, there were high demands that this be done in a reliable, predictable and legally secure manner; if this was not the case, there was a risk that society's trust in the system would be damaged. In this context, a knee-jerk reaction – or relying on someone else to react – can pose significant risks and difficulties in implementation. Changes in this particular sector must therefore be made with great care and in dialogue with citizens and stakeholders affected by the changes.

What digitalization is

Digital solutions were a frequent option as a response to the restrictions imposed by the pandemic. These solutions allow for remote communication and interaction, which is what the restrictions often resulted in. Digitalization thus became a solution to the problem and a prerequisite for the continued functioning of our societies and industries. But when we talk about digitalization, and the digital transformation of society as a whole, it is important to remember that digitalization does not mean the same thing for everyone, and that it appears in different ways in different contexts, with different digital technologies having different relevance in different industries (see, for instance, Browning et al, 2022). Digitalization is thus a broad concept that can include a variety of different technologies, tools and ideas. In the initial phase of the pandemic, it was perhaps information and communication technologies that were crucial to the ability of organizations to adapt to a remote working life, but in general it can be said that digitalization is about implementing any digital technologies or processes to create value, while digital transformation is the process and the resulting changes in society and industry.

A number of digital technologies are particularly relevant in the legal field. Some of these are information and communication technologies – new ways of communicating but also of managing and analysing large amounts of data. There is also a strong focus on artificial intelligence (AI) in the legal field. AI can be seen as both a great opportunity and a great challenge. This is because legal knowledge and services have long been reserved for human intelligence and skills and are also knowledge intensive in the sense that human skills (and human capital) were previously sufficient to produce the service. This has led to the emergence of a system based on the valuation of law in time. We buy and value legal services *by the hour*. And for hours, there is a natural limitation for us humans. Even if a lawyer's week is not necessarily limited to 40 hours, there are only 24 hours in a day, and at some point you have to sleep. However, AI does not have this limitation, which means there is an incredible opportunity for value creation. And with increased production of law, in other ways than through an investment in human capital, the service can also be priced differently.

If we succeeded in creating the conditions to produce legal knowledge and legal services without being constrained by human labour time and cognitive abilities, we could produce law 24/7 and at a lower cost. In this way, law could be priced differently and reach many more people. This is what is often referred to as a democratization of the law. In other words, digital technologies have the potential to create legal services more efficiently, making law more accessible and cheaper. This does not require advanced AI. A legal system based on automation and more accurate information management would suffice. But claiming that we can replace the professional lawyer, or judge, with an artificial colleague also creates friction in the industry (Kronblad and Pregmark, 2021). There is much pride in legal knowledge – where knowledge is power – a strong professional identity and a strong professional organization that has much to gain from keeping power structures and hierarchies as they are. This works in harmony with business models that are based on hours. At the same time, hourly based models are at odds with digitalization, which is itself presented as a time-saving process. This creates a conflict between different business perspectives when digitalization now enters the law as a means of enabling essential telework (which I will return to later in the chapter).

That digitalization looks different in different industries and in different contexts is something that I gained greater insight into when I conducted a research study on the difference in digitalization between professional fields, in which I focused on the difference between the legal industry and architecture. In the field of architecture, digitalization was very much a question of increased opportunities to use new tools for digital sketching, but it was also about being able to create models of buildings through additive manufacturing, about building information modelling and about creating digital twins. An important lesson I took away was how digitalization here created completely new business models and financial flows. The architects told me that being able to render images directly from the drawings meant that they now had access to such realistic images that the projects could be sold directly. Suddenly, for example, the building did not have to be constructed for the apartments in it to be sold.

This transformed the financial flows in the industry and provided opportunities to finance construction in new ways, which also created new conditions in the financial infrastructure. Another revolutionary example comes from the construction industry, where the possibility, and emergence of, smart cities means that we can combine digitalization with ambitions for social and environmental sustainability. In this type of initiative and project, we benefit from connectivity, networked thinking (internet of things) and the ability to use and analyse large amounts of data to control flows and transport of, for example, people, goods and energy.

The implementation of the technology thus creates the conditions for social change. And how things look in similar, or neighbouring, industries often has a bearing on the industry you are focusing on. So also in this case, for example, in the rapid transition to virtual courts, we can see that it is not only information and communication technologies that are relevant to enable the transition but also the technologies that I came across in my study on archiving, with increasingly effective tools based on *virtual* and *augmented* reality.

Although the transformation we now find ourselves in did not come with the pandemic, COVID-19 accelerated an already ongoing shift where professional work, in a wide range of industries, had already begun. In *The Second Machine Age*, Brynjolfsson and McAfee (2014) talk about this ongoing shift, stating that we are in a 'new machine age' in which machines are increasingly replacing humans. While the first machine age was about an industrial transformation where agricultural and manufacturing workers were increasingly being replaced by computing power and various machines and robots, we are now in an era where analytical and creative skills can also be replaced. And it was in this ongoing transition that the pandemic struck, affecting both the scale and speed of the transition. Thus, it was not only the pandemic that affected our courts but the fact this happened at a time when the digital transformation of both the industry and the courts had already begun. In an increasingly digitalized society, lawyers – including lawyers, family lawyers, prosecutors and judges – are faced with new issues and new means of evidence. Since lawyers have this role in order to solve problems in other industries, they must keep up with the digital transition and create an understanding of the new issues that arise (Kronblad, 2021).

A shift to digital ways of working

When COVID-19 struck, much of society went into lockdown. To reduce the spread of infection, we were banished to our homes, while public spaces and buildings were emptied. This lockdown took place to varying degrees across the world. In fact, Sweden is one of the countries that had the gentlest lockdown: schools, as well as many critical societal institutions (such as our courts), remained open. I was able to follow this transition through a research project at an administrative court that a colleague and I had started even before the outbreak of COVID-19. This court contacted us in 2019 and asked us to help them on their digitalization journey, as they felt the pace of change was too slow. They felt there were many obstacles along the way, and they were not getting the leverage on the implementation of digital tools and processes that management wanted. We went to the court to observe the work of, and interview, a number of judges and other employees about the challenges and opportunities they perceived in the new digital ways of working. In these early interviews, it was clear there was widespread resistance to digitalization, which mainly appeared as something that management was trying to speed up and push into the business without having the judges on board. Those we interviewed highlighted that there were major security risks, that the software and platforms were too poor, that they did not have the right skills, that management also lacked digital skills and, finally, that they did not want to change their working methods – as they 'like to work on paper'. In many organizations, these types of barriers could be overcome by a common approach, but in the courts there is an additional difficulty in achieving homogeneous working practices, as judges have a lot of freedom in how they perform their tasks. This means that the chief judge in each unit largely determines the nature of the work processes. Thus, prior to the pandemic, there was frustration among management that digitalization was proceeding very slowly, and strong resistance in the organization (Björkdahl and Kronblad, 2021).

Then came the pandemic. For a while, our research project was put on hold; there were many other things to focus on. But a year later, we went back to the court and made new observations and conducted new interviews, and suddenly a whole new picture emerged. Now the digital processes were in place, and the judges were working on the digital platforms without resistance. They had not only accepted the new digital ways of working but also had a positive perception of them and were in favour of further digital transformation.

When we started investigating this, in order to understand what had brought about this rapid acceptance, we found that although all the technology had been available at the court before COVID-19, it was being marketed internally as a change to create efficiency and time savings. This was not something the judges cared much about. Time savings and efficiency are not high on the list of judges' professional goals. Quality, on the other hand – delivering quality, and ensuring that justice is delivered regardless of time constraints – is a valid justification. In addition, the chief judges were keen to ensure that employees in their particular departments had the best working conditions. When the restrictions came into force, those chief judges who had introduced digital work processes in their departments were able to allow their employees to work from home and thus protect them from infection, while those who could not ensure legally secure digital work processes were not able to protect their employees from infection – they had to come in to work. With this change came a new justification for digitalization: it was no longer a question of digitalization for the sake of digitalization but of digitalization motivated by protecting employees from infection. And this was something the judges were able to accept. As more and more departments began to test digital practices and tools in this way, they realized that it might not be as bad as they thought. They quickly learned how to manage security risks and understood that digitalization brought not only efficiency gains but also quality gains. Before the pandemic, one judge likened the situation to standing on the edge of a pool and not wanting to jump in – 'someone has to push us in' for things to happen. And maybe that's exactly what the pandemic did. It pushed the whole organization into the pool. But what made it work – that the employees started swimming instead of drowning – was probably the preparations that had been made, and that all the conditions for digital work were already in place. Management had simply given employees the right conditions to learn to swim quickly. But what happens now? Do we get out of the pool? Will there be a backlash and a return to old ways of working and habits, or have we created 'the new normal' that we will stay in? At the court, they talked a lot about what they wanted to keep, and the ability to work remotely was one such thing (at least when needed). But they also reflected on what was lost when they were not on site. The same reflections were made at a workshop I held for a group of about 80 Court of Appeal judges in October 2021. The President of the Court of Appeal opened the day with the following words: 'The pandemic has made us adopt new ways of working, but now it is time to evaluate and see what we want to keep. Today we will capitalize on each other's wisdom.' The point was that many decisions were rushed in the rapid digitalization process that followed the pandemic, and even though many of the changes introduced were positive, there was a lot that was rushed, a lot of cobbled-together solutions that worked for the moment but would not last in the longer term. The best way to find the right solutions was to take a step back and evaluate with open eyes what had worked and what had not. During this day, we also reflected on the fact that Sweden had not completely switched to virtual trials and that this was unique compared to other countries.

What did change, however, was that the court allowed remote presence for certain parties in order to avoid cancelling the entire trial if a party, witness or judge was ill. This involved an individual connecting to the courtroom via their mobile phone or a computer from home. The judges thought this had worked very well, and it was seen as a great benefit to society not to have to cancel the court processes completely. However, there was some scepticism about using digital appearances in all types of cases. It was felt, for example, that in certain juvenile cases, there was a benefit in bringing the young criminal suspect to court. Knowing that the adult world has seen that you have committed an offence, investigated it and holds you responsible can bring home the seriousness of the situation. The court has an educational purpose here, in which location and ceremonial elements are important. Just by being there, you realize the importance of the court as a social institution.

But apart from these juvenile cases, the judges did not really see many disadvantages of a digital setting. A telling feature of this workshop was that the conversation instead focused on the benefits of digitalization: how much more flexible their work had become and how the processes had become more efficient and enabled clearer control and faster decisions. In addition, we talked a lot about the digital developments that had taken place during the pandemic (a couple of years is oceans of time when we talk about technological developments), such as digital file management, digital judgments and using AI for translations in the court process. So, instead of talking about a return to the status quo, we discussed how we could further improve the digital transformation, how we could increase the quality and security of the services provided to the public.

The voices heard were unanimously positive. Thus, it seems that my conclusions from the local court hold true in general: when forced to test the digital ways of working, people re-evaluate them, breaking down previous barriers and creating openings for a continued digitalization journey.

I believe that the rapid digitalization opened the door for further changes in general and that we have now entered on a path that we will not, or even cannot, reverse. In an article I wrote together with Johanna Pregmark, we talk about the emergence of a 'corona bump on the digital trajectory' and say that even if organizations take steps back, after COVID-19 has disappeared and the restrictions are over, the organizations' starting point is at a higher level on their development curves, as they are more digital than before. This means both a shift in the curve, so that the starting point is now higher up, and that the development in the future is expected to be faster (a steeper curve). This faster pace reflects both exponential digital development and the organization's increased ability to change, which has now been improved because the organization has practised change. We are therefore unlikely to go back to the way things were, although some practices will return. Instead, we can say that we have reached a new normal of higher digitalization. The bouncing back effect is thus expected to be limited.

Varieties of virtual courts around the world

As I have already mentioned, the changes looked different for courts in different countries. There were also different legal conditions for holding trials entirely digitally. In Sweden, for example, there is a requirement for processes to be public, while at the same time we have a ban on recording: you are not allowed to film or photograph in court. In the United States, there is a similar requirement with regard to publicity, but it is not combined with a ban on recording, which enabled a transition to YouTube-broadcast trials (Sourdin et al, 2020) (which would not have been possible in Sweden). In China, several completely virtual courts were established (such as the Beijing Internet Court), which enabled a completely digital court process from filing to ruling and mediation to be conducted online. This system operates 24/7 and can thus handle a large number of cases. The parties in the various cases attend the court via WeChat, which is a leading social media platform in China. The use of a platform that requires access only to a mobile phone and not to a computer is seen as a great strength in its capability to reach out to the masses (Sourdin, 2020). Brazil also went far in its virtual transformation. Here, most of the work was converted to digital work in many of the higher courts. At the same time, courts in major cities moved to virtual trials. However, digital maturity varied across the country, and local courts faced very different challenges in the transition: some residents simply did not have access to the technology (smartphones, for example) that would have enabled them to go digital. This meant that a large number of trials in rural areas had to be cancelled (AJUFE, 2022).

This in turn means that what is known as the digital divide is growing, and growing in importance. The difference between those individuals (and places) who have access to technological infrastructure, digital technology and the skills to use it and those who do not thus becomes crucial to their access to justice. This is an unfair and unfortunate development that needs to be addressed in the wake of the pandemic. However, it should be noted that these cancelled cases did not necessarily lead to the consequences, and extended waiting times, that were initially envisaged, as the need for court services (almost) coincided with the restrictions. When communities were closed down, there were initially fewer incidences of drunkenness, brawls and traffic offences that otherwise create the minor criminal cases that occupy a significant part of the court's resources.

Regardless of which and how many cases came to the courts, the lawyers and judges were not as ready to jump on the digital train. Some courts did not even have digital systems but still relied solely on paper handling. Some had digital case management systems, while others found themselves in a situation where they had to quickly adapt to remote working. However, this took less time for them, as they were able to quickly implement the systems that other courts had already tested and verified. Some had installed and were using digital conferencing tools, but certainly not all. However, when the pandemic struck and the need arose, things moved quickly: new video conferencing tools such as Teams, Skype, Zoom, Google Hangouts and Webex were installed and started to be used (Sourdin et al, 2020).

It was also common to move to different types of hybrid trials in which some elements were digital, or allowed for a digital presence, as in Sweden (with digital presence for some parties). These tools, which were increasingly used, were not in themselves major innovations. I am talking here about relatively simple technologies and tools that were largely implemented as a direct translation from their analogue counterparts. However, when put in context, their implementation represents an enormous institutional change. By implementing different digital tools and processes simultaneously, the court went from being bound to the place, and to the material, to being something else. Suddenly, justice became a service that could be delivered online and in new ways. This is a significant institutional change and one that creates an opportunity for further innovation and change. Justice as a Service (JaaS) is thus also becoming a reality in the judicial world. JaaS is a term that is usually used to talk about private companies that target the consumer market in various ways in order to help them resolve their disputes. Examples include AirHelp, which helps people get compensation after cancelled and delayed flights, or Pixsy, which helps individuals sue for unauthorized use of photographs. There is now also an opening for public justice to be distributed in similar (simple) ways via digital channels, and this presents an opportunity for the democratization of justice. Justice can suddenly be created and distributed at a lower cost and thus become available to more people.

Algorithmic (in)justice

However, not everything about the digital transformation is positive. As society changes and becomes increasingly digital, digital components are also becoming more common in the cases that the courts handle. These may involve complex digital legal issues, such as liability for an accident caused by a self-driving car or a robot that malfunctions during surgery. It can also involve incorrect positioning data from mobile phone masts or incorrectly coded algorithmic decision-making systems that generate incorrect decisions. My current research concerns just such a case: the application of an algorithmic decision system for the placement of school pupils. In this case, where the code was clearly incorrect and in violation of law and practice, I tested the legal system's ability to handle digital issues and digital evidence. In 2020, I sued the City of Gothenburg (within the framework of a research project) for not complying with the Education Act (2010:800) and the Municipal Act (2017:72) when coding and implementing an algorithmic decision-making system for the placement of 12,000 children in primary school. Gothenburg had created a system that placed the children in the nearest school as the crow flies, without considering how close the school actually was given their walking and cycling distance to it. In Gothenburg, with a cityscape dominated by a wide river that divides the city in two, this created several hundred incorrect placements. Children were placed on the opposite side of the river from their home, in schools that the algorithm counted as 'close' but which in reality meant an hour-long commute.

The system also prioritized geographical parameters, while the school choices made by parents were not even coded. This was also in violation of the law. The errors made by the primary school administration were confirmed by a report from the city audit in 2021, but by then I had already lost the case. When it went to court in 2020, they found that analyses of the results (where the children were placed) were not enough to prove that the procedure was illegal. And because the city never disclosed the code they used, these errors were impossible to prove. The system's legality could therefore not be tested, and that risk fell on me as the applicant, who thus had the burden of proof for the claim that the decision-making process was unlawful. The consequence of this (the court's inability to deal adequately with the issues of evidence) is that some 700 children are still (2022) attending schools where they would not have been placed had the algorithmic decision-making system been coded correctly and legally. In my view, this is a clear case of algorithmic injustice where the courts lack the expertise and institutional tools to deal with new digital societal problems. And when the courts cannot handle the issues and problems that arise, we can no longer claim to have the rule of law. Of course, this could be solved. This could, however, be solved through a combination of increased competence and adaptations of procedural law so that it better reflects, and can handle, the digital age in which we live.

But, it is a major challenge, if not almost impossible, to increase the digital competence of all courts and judges, as digital components and digital evidence can now be found in all types of cases. Today, the courts are organized according to their geographical jurisdictions, which means that cases are handled in a local court and are also appealed against in superior courts that reflect the geography of Sweden. To handle the digital cases (and cases with advanced digital evidence), we would need to enable a different type of organization, for example that certain courts would no longer reflect a geographical catchment area but instead a certain expertise. And this is where virtual courts can offer a solution.

Thus, there is an opportunity in the virtual court to organize for justice in new ways. When geography does not impose restrictions on how courts must be organized, the possibility of organizing the judiciary in new ways arises, and this provides an opportunity to solve the growing problem of algorithmic injustice. Suddenly, there would be a space to create specialist courts, which could, for example, specialize in cases with digital complexity or digital evidence. This would make it possible to have judges who are, or become, experts in understanding code and digital complexity in a legal context. Virtual courts both open a mental space for such a change and create a practical space where this can happen.

Digitalization of law?

The transformation of the judiciary that was reinforced and accelerated during the pandemic meant that legal processes were increasingly handled digitally. A range of new practices, as well as new opportunities, were invented. These changes are not unique to law but are similar across a wide range of professional fields; however, what is so special about the rapid and profound change in the world of justice is that before the pandemic it had remained unchanged for a very long time. After centuries of slow evolution of the institutions of law, we have now experienced almost a digital revolution, a revolution that affects not only practices and the way things are but also how we experience and view them. If one can suddenly imagine court processes becoming digital and virtual, it is likely that many other areas will follow.

Accepting this significant change in the justice system opens the door to a greater acceptance of change in general, which influences and enables other institutional change. Moving from seeing the court as a place to seeing it as a service is a significant mind shift that opens up all sorts of other changes. Digitalization presents a significant opportunity to deliver effective justice in a modern world, reducing the number of slow processes and creating cheaper and more accessible legal services. This could be particularly important for those groups in society that are already vulnerable; it will be a democratization of justice, where justice at a distance and justice as a service become two important components.

11

Organizing Welfare under Extraordinary Circumstances

In the study on which this book is based, we have been exploring how various professions/occupations in the public sector carried out their tasks in circumstances that were completely new. But we have also noticed that the extraordinary situation created by COVID-19 affected the relationship between professions closest to the core of welfare activities and organizations that house their activities. The general question is, therefore, how the public sector was organized and governed in times of dramatic and transformative events, and whether this sector, and the rest of society, have developed preparedness for future crises. What happens when ordinary economic, political and labour law conditions for public activities become limited or redefined? Did national and regional authorities, municipalities and welfare units have the capacity to function in such such extraordinary circumstances?

The pandemic and (un)organized professional work

The framework that helped us to understand how people in various professions and occupations dealt with the pandemic was a focus on the interactions between such professions and formal organizations that created the conditions for the work of public employees. This interaction mainly concerned such issues as space, opportunity, knowledge and skills, enabling them to influence the forms and content of welfare work as they needed to be adapted to the demands that arose in the wake of the pandemic. A picture of the role of our interviewees and their organizations during the years of COVID-19 that emerges from the accounts we collected can be summarized as what Ahrne and Papakostas (2002) describe as 'organizational inertia'. Such inertia, or sluggishness, can be interpreted as an inability or an unwillingness to adapt to changes in an organization's environment. It was by leaders and their subordinates often having different perceptions of what these changes should look like. In the management literature, such inertia is usually attributed to the subordinates, while studies of public sector organizations reveal that it is more often the formal organization that produces inertia (Ahrne and Papakostas, 2002).

We have analysed this inertia by dividing the relationships between civil servants and the leadership of their formal organizations during the pandemic into different phases. These phases correspond both to the chronological development of the pandemic (and hence to the division of chapters in the first part of the book) and to changes in public servants' views on the response of their organizations to the efforts and adaptations made by employees in their work.

Phase 1: autonomy and inevitable resistance

The design and adaptation of daily work during the initial phase of the pandemic was largely the responsibility of front line personnel. Many interviewees told us how they had to quickly adapt to the new situation while their organization lacked procedures, knowledge, experience and information to help them carry on their core mission. People had to rely on their own thoughts and skills to find solutions to the problems that arose with the advent of COVID-19. The new situation permitted more autonomous actions and a partial decoupling from formal procedures, requirements and expectations. Of course, this did not apply to all employees and was not experienced in all places where we conducted our interviews. Some municipalities and some organizations had previous comparable experiences from, for example, the refugee crisis in 2015, or the wildfires in the summer of 2018. In other places, there was enough time and insight to create basic preparedness in the form of guidelines, procedures and the purchase of IT and protective equipment. Even in such places, however, most interviewees testified to a relatively large distance between management functions and what was happening 'on the ground'. This distance was often physical, as managers in schools, care homes or municipal administrations were able to work from home more often than others. But our interlocutors also talked about organizational distance, where heads of operations, heads of units, municipal leaders and politicians seemed to inhabit a different reality, where the pandemic was not as present and tangible:

> The director of culture tells us from the screen – 'now go home to your families, don't be alone' – as you might say to somebody with a cancer diagnosis – 'and if you have any questions, go to your manager. Go to your manager, go to the person who has made a career here' – in the short time they have been here – 'and don't sit here, don't answer emails, don't walk around the premises, don't attend meetings ...' The

> result is that the whole workforce becomes anxious and confused. (B9, line manager, West South)

These somewhat harsh comments and conclusions point to the frustration that people in various welfare professions and occupations experienced due to what was perceived as weak support from management staff. It also suggests that employees had to find their own solutions to the problems that arose in the early days of the pandemic, as these were outside the frame of formal work processes, routines and support structures. Quite often, employees saw their own leaders, local government departments or individual welfare organizations as paralysed. In some municipalities, the technical equipment necessary for a rapid transition to telework was lacking, as was knowledge of how new digital systems could be used in an efficient and legally secure manner:

> That process [of getting the equipment necessary for working remotely] was slow in the beginning. We do have laptops, but you can't very often sit and work on your screen. ... We are a fairly centralized authority ... because it is not our unit as such that owns this process, but it is owned centrally, and we must have an OK for everything from there. The wheels there were turning a little too slowly, I think ... But once it got going, it was OK to take the equipment home; you just had to fill in and send in a form. (B32, head of office, Central East)

Such difficulties were not experienced everywhere. In some places, the staff's first steps into pandemic management were facilitated by quick action 'on the buying side'. Thus, while procedures and organizational support were relatively weak, there was at least technical equipment: 'The equipment is much better now. Before corona, we didn't have laptops or good mobile phones. Now we got them at the very beginning. There has been talk about us getting them for years, but nothing has ever happened before' (C1, social secretary, North).

Getting the technology into place was one thing, but knowing how to use it was another. For some, the transition to telework and digitalized working life was a matter of inventing new ways of handling their tasks. The IT manager in West municipality pointed to this difference, noting that at the beginning of the pandemic, the knowledge and procedures for using digital technologies did not keep up with their acquisition and implementation:

> For our part, corona has been positive, I would say. On the one hand, digitalization has received a boost as we have advocated it. But it has been difficult to achieve, both politically and at the operational level. ... Since we have achieved this computerization [during the first

> period of the pandemic], people have realized that they can work from home – meetings are [now] run in a completely different way. ... As for the politicians, we needed to teach them about digital meetings. They have made the biggest journey, and they they've done really well! (C9, IT manager, West)

Welfare officers in South Central municipality were of the same opinion. At first, there were few standard work processes and routines where digital technology would be of help. The staff themselves had to think about how the new tools would be used:

> We became very good at the digital aspect ... making it work at meetings, on home visits, on follow-ups and the like. Because we were often the ones who went to the client's home and had a computer with us, while the others, nurses, doctors and other colleagues, sat at the computer. We really developed our ability to hold a digital meeting ... and to get everyone to be active even though they were sitting at their screens. Our ability to work quickly was also helped by the digital equipment. (D12, counsellor, South Central)

Phase 2: quest for control and reduced professional space

Staff and professions often saw the (partly enforced) freedom as a necessity to meet the challenges posed by the pandemic. Yet an equally common interpretation was that this freedom challenged an organizational status quo, producing a stalemate over who should determine the content and form of work necessary for delivering public services, and how. In this context, managers were seen as more active and present compared to the first phase. For them, it was a question of how the organizations should relate to the adaptations and solutions generated by staff dealing with the challenges of the pandemic. The head of West municipality described what happened when solutions to emerging problems were solved by professionals themselves:

> If you start at the bottom of the chain, you'll notice that people get the chance to take many good initiatives. I can take the example of an assistant nurse who was given the task of managing the central equipment store, and it was very cleverly organized. What do you do if you need a visor, like in home care? They realized that you could have a bucket with the equipment and hand sanitizer with which you could clean anything that was needed, and then put the lid on the bucket. So solutions like these were very opportune. Also, there were librarians who realized that maybe the library didn't have to be open,

> maybe they could send out books in another way. (C19, municipal manager, West)

Yet, from a management perspective, such adaptations and solutions sometimes meant that in many respects staff deviated from the structures and decision-making paths that existed in pre-pandemic organizations. Such deviations were more obvious in some places:

> The managerial know-how also contains an expectation of doing things strictly by the book. After all, no one should be able to say that the university ignores laws and regulations! So the hierarchical order kicks in quickly in a crisis, and there was a certain amount of anxiety about the changes and their consequences. Departmental board meetings were cancelled at the last minute rather than being moved online. (B14, university lecturer, Central)

In some other workplaces, management staff took a more reflective and relaxed approach to the formal organization, even with regard to their own activities. Also, trust in the knowledge and skills of staff was highlighted as the basis for successful management of the pandemic, especially when important priorities had to be set:

> [L]eadership in a crisis is very much based on having a well-structured, functioning organization with daily trust; trust in various professions and trust in each other. That makes it so much easier. For example, I know that we have state and regional authorities and county councils and so on, that they all demand many different planning documents. But they were not the ones that helped us move forward. They are there and they should be there, but they are not what has helped us. The fact is that we have a decent organization that works with trust-based management and steering, an organization that has the ability to understand and say, 'No, let's put other things aside and prioritize that.' That was the lesson. I know what is in our pandemic plan, and the updated pandemic plan, but I haven't looked at it very often to be honest. That was not the success factor. (D11, municipal director, Central South)

This quote can also be read as an expression of the management's desire to be an active part of the changes and adaptations that originated from the staff's handling of problems and challenges outside the framework of the formal organization. In our conversations with municipal directors and heads of functional units, we also observed that they seemed to be looking for their own place in pandemic management – especially when the most obvious pandemic response had to come from the professions and occupations closest to the users of public services. While managers tried to support and assist their staff in their work, they also reflected on their own tasks and the responsibilities of their organizations:

> It is difficult to do developmental work right now, so we need to look a little more at how we should go forward. Because it's not as if digital meetings are the forum for creativity. Yes, there is a lot that can be done, and I have tried to do various things, like digital brainstorming. But it isn't as good as a meeting with sticky-it notes. (B30, head of education, Central)

On several occasions, management staff also spoke about activities that were more about supporting the formal structures, cooperation (for example between managers, individual municipal operations or entire municipalities), communication and the preparation of crisis and contingency plans rather than being directly involved in the specific work of the welfare professions. As several interviewees pointed out, it was difficult to find ways 'to be close' to those who performed the core tasks:

> I have been influenced by the fact that people in my organization have found it so incredibly positive to be able to work from home, and so I have settled for it. But now when I look back, I wish I had put more focus on relationship building, much more than I have done. (D7, social services manager, Central South)

Phase 3: towards increased formalization

This phase mainly involved staff in the state and municipal services performing their work in accordance with formal structures, procedures and plans in contrast to the activities their organizations had developed in response to what occurred during the first phases. It can also be claimed that welfare staff in the various professions and occupations lost some of their initial mandate to shape and restructure their work tasks:

> We got the municipal council and the municipal board to work together very, very well from the start, despite the chaos. But we still improved it along the way. In the beginning, we had to improvise ... but quite quickly we felt that we needed more routines. ... Within the municipality, there was a structure suitable for this task and many functional units within the staff were involved in developing new procedures. (C3, municipal secretary, North)

The new formal structures and procedures were seen as proof that authorities, municipalities and various municipal organizations were catching up with developments that were partly beyond their control in the early stages of the pandemic. There was now an opportunity for learning and creating preparedness for new waves of the pandemic, for example by formalizing new procedures for digital meetings:

> I don't know what it's like in other offices, but I believe that the lessons and working methods learnt will be taken on board now that the pandemic is over. The question is which new procedures we have put in place it might be good to keep or modify. We may not go back to the way things were before. Instead, we are thinking about whether there is something good in the new procedures, so we will be sticking to certain things. (C5, administrative manager, North)

A formalization of the spontaneous ways of working that were typical at the beginning of the pandemic was met with disappointment by some and with relief by others. As we have suggested in previous chapters, a lack of adequate support and information about what, when and how to do the work led to high levels of stress. This stress was reduced when organizations and their management were given more control over the new activities, thus making it easier to focus on the task at hand. Although this could mean a loss of control over daily work and sometimes led to a reduction of democratic elements in how the municipalities planned and implemented some of their activities, resistance to increased formalization was relatively limited:

> During the pandemic we also experienced more concern from above about what we did. We were simply not allowed to decide for ourselves what to post on social media or on our common web. Instead, it was 'now it's this, now it's this wording'. The municipality's communication department got involved and they were the ones who decided, who put together what should be written and where. We had to wait and publish this on such and such a date, and make sure it was formulated in the right way. So there was a completely different kind of control than the usual one, when we believed we had the autonomy to publish information ... it became more regulated and more visible from above during this period, definitely. (D3, library coordinator, Central South)

Others perceived this move towards a normal regime as a return to a state where professional knowledge and experience were less relevant. Managers were among those wondered what their work would look like when the pandemic no longer required extraordinary efforts and profession-specific knowledge were, paradoxically, some managers.

All in all, the increased formalization that characterized the third phase was based on the tension between the people closest to the core tasks of the operations and the administrative officials who became even more influential during the pandemic. Their role grew at the expense of the professional practice of staff, whose scope for taking responsibility for and shaping the content and form of their work became limited. This newfound autonomy became increasingly subordinate to formal steering.

Managing professional work in a crisis: everything is new, and everything is the same as before

The stories we heard during the final stages of the pandemic reinforced the picture of a development through which formal organizations once again emerged as key elements of public activities. The room for manoeuvre and the occasions when professional judgement guided the management of the pandemic continued to diminish. Thus, in many respects, public services were moving towards what can be characterized as pre-pandemic governance. When asked about the future that loomed beyond the horizons of the pandemic, some doubted that the benefits that the pandemic had brought to their work could be sustained:

> We need to keep the positive things that came up during the pandemic! But I believe that this is one of the biggest puzzles we have to solve. We haven't seen a lot of new inventions during this pandemic. There were no consultants coming to sell us something, because there was no one they could meet. Everything has been put on hold – and that has been fantastic. (D4, social secretary, Central South)

Others expressed hope that the management staff would hurry to turn the municipal operations back to old, proven routines, and such a view was not unusual during this phase. While teachers, librarians, social workers, administrators and others related to formal governance as something more or less inevitable and as a non-optional framing of their work, school principals, municipal directors and various operational managers were convinced that it was the formal structures, routines and guidelines that were the prerequisites for staff to be able to perform their work during the crisis:

> I think that, hopefully, management in general has an arrangement in place for such events, so that we can return to the old way of working fairly quickly. ... when there is a structure and routines for this, it should be much easier to just say [snaps fingers]: 'Let's do this again.' (D9, administrative assistant, Central South)

An analysis of the four phases reveals at least two trends in how the public sector responded to the pandemic. On the one hand, people in various welfare professions and occupations showed considerable resilience and competence in dealing with the new and unfamiliar challenges brought about by COVID. On the other hand, managers attempted to capture, control and formalize these challenges and make them follow historically established practices and governance perspectives. These two trends both overlapped and conflicted with each other:

> [I]t becomes a bit 'more of the same' ... a confirmation of how things usually work in society and in the municipal sector. I'm not saying that politicians and municipal leaders don't care – because they do. But they are incapable of truly addressing what staff have done in an adequate way. In the end, it's all reduced to the fact that 'we did a good job' because we can tick certain boxes. Still, we were damn lucky they didn't go any other way. (D17, teacher, South East)

How personnel approached the pandemic can be explained by their previously acquired expertise and the ability to make independent judgements and adaptations based on this expertise. Coupled with work ethics and practice based on personal sacrifice, flexibility, sympathy and a blend of personal and professional life, health professionals, teachers, social workers, administrators and others demonstrated that they could independently adapt existing practices and invent new ones to continue their work. This was particularly evident in the early months of the pandemic, when professional resilience – the ability to practise one's profession under limited material and organizational conditions – was central to ensuring the continuity and stability of welfare provision:

> We have 50 employees in our retirement home and one unit manager. But the head of the unit certainly isn't the only one with a brain. You have to reason with your staff ... It helps if someone in the group – or the manager – has been through a crisis before. But if they haven't, there should be an administrative function for this purpose ... It shouldn't be us, the heads of administration, who are in that group, it should be those who are best suited to such tasks – perhaps the head of the education administration should be there. You have to be able to define the target, and make an analysis, and for this we need communication and collaboration. This is the management function. (D20, deputy municipal director, Central North)

There was a considerable variation in how the changes resulting from professional adaptation to the pandemic were addressed and supported in different organizational contexts. This variation can be linked both to the size and type of the organizations and to the development of the pandemic in the immediate geographical vicinity. A common feature seemed to be that although municipalities and state authorities tried to support staff in various welfare professions at the beginning of the pandemic, the underlying inertia in the formal governance, administration and organization of the work of these professions also intensified in time.

To summarize the most important lessons we learned about the governance and organization of public welfare services and the professions and occupations within them, in the following chapter we introduce the concept of *pandemicracy*.

12

Pandemicracy

The studies mentioned in this book's introduction gave us no reason to suspect that our material would point in a radically different direction. Although these earlier studies were based on material from health and social care organizations, and schools in particular, there are similarities between the experiences of staff and professionals 'behind the front line' and those 'beyond the spotlight'. Our interviewees, similarly to healthcare professionals, point to commitment and professional expertise as crucial to the continued functioning of our shared welfare services. Their stories highlighted the need to learn how to deal with challenges associated with a lack of organizational and communicative preparedness as well as a shortage of resources and necessary equipment.

However, we also found interesting differences, partly because we studied other organizations and professions, but also because our interviews and observations spanned across almost three years, which allowed us to notice events and aspects of the responses to the pandemic that become clearer only when viewed from a longer time perspective. The nature and character of relations between welfare professionals and their organizations as we have described them in previous chapters is one such aspect. Another aspect concerns the administrative and political processes that were challenged during the pandemic, partly because of the measures and actions implemented by municipalities, government agencies and central authorities. As highlighted by Bergmann and Lindström (2023), Sweden's approach, characterized by its reliance on recommendations rather than strict mandates, tested the resilience and flexibility of its democratic ideals. While this strategy emphasized individual responsibility, it also revealed tensions between public health policies and the democratic underpinning of these. Since we see administration (a central part of how public organizations organize their tasks) and democracy (that is, the overarching principles on the basis of which the tasks of public organizations are to be interpreted) as interlinked and to some extent also dependent on each other, we will discuss these two subsequently as expressions of what we have chosen to call pandemicracy.[1] Using this concept, we seek to describe both the solutions that the governance-oriented administration (bureaucracy) developed as a response to the pandemic and the forms of expression through which these solutions characterized the social anchoring and mission of municipalities and authorities (democracy).

Pandemic and governance

Large parts of the Swedish welfare sector are framed in extensive administrative structures, routines and practices, and these usually limit the ability of welfare professionals to determine the form and content of their work. We see the introduction and spread of various management models and perspectives aimed at controlling, evaluating and standardizing the work of welfare professionals as one of the explanations of why the public sector is poorly equipped to deal with unexpected events and crises. Organizations in this sector rely on governance through the formal hierarchy and associated administration, rather than the ability of their employees to make independent decisions and evaluate different tasks based on their professional judgement (Styhre, 2013; Bornemark, 2020). Unsurprisingly, this type of governance was inevitably challenged and seen as less relevant, especially in contexts where administration and bureaucracy stood in the way of the adjustments that needed to be made in the early months of the pandemic. In this way, professionals involved in teaching, care, supervision or counselling were given (and sometimes created) more room for manoeuvre, where formal governance was less tangible and coercive. Our material is rich in illustrations where, for example, the lack of protective and technical equipment, inappropriate spatial arrangements or the absence of middle and senior management meant that the work and tasks of welfare professionals had to be reorganized and designed on the basis of their own reasoning, understanding, considerations and assessments.

However, while the existing forms of governance in some contexts led the welfare professionals to follow formal regulations, norms and guidelines to a lesser extent, there were situations where the reverse was true. The adaptation that municipal secretaries, social workers, teachers, environmental inspectors, administrators and operation managers, among others, needed to make to cope with the transition to digital routines contributed to these groups having to do more administrative work, albeit in partly novel ways. In professions where teleworking was more common, there was also an emphasis on the creation of, and compliance with, routines and working methods that were more in line with the governance methods that the professions were used to from the time before the pandemic. In this context, it would, of course, be unfair to argue that bureaucracy only stood in the way and weakened their efforts. As we have seen in the chapters on schools, libraries and courts, governance systems were also highly functional and could create external – legal and principled – frameworks that certain professions could lean on to ensure, among other things, legally secure, predictable and uninterrupted exercise of authority and the provision of welfare services. This picture is also confirmed in other studies where municipalities' management of the pandemic showed both adaptability and resilience, not least thanks to local autonomy and decentralization (Kuhlmann et al, 2021; Brorström and Löfström, 2022).

There is also a third approach to formal administration and governance of public sector organizations, which was most evident among management staff. In much the same way as we described in our previous study on the governance of municipal elderly care (Jernberg and Pallas, 2022), administrative personnel in management functions also used the pandemic to gain even more control over the various activities that were part of their municipalities and authorities. At the same time, they sought (and obtained) a more autonomous role in relation to the local government and municipal political bodies. This shift in power over decisions about what should be done, by whom and how became even more apparent during the pandemic. The shift is directly linked to the final theme of our book: how pandemic management may have come to challenge the democratic mission of municipalities and local authorities, and the democratic processes in which these organizations are a central part.

The pandemic and local democracy

Through their status as public organizations, and through their tasks as bearers of central democratic processes and principles, government agencies and municipalities must comply with and maintain the legislation that is the foundation of a democratic society. This applies not only to general constitutions and laws such as the principle of public access to information, freedom of expression and freedom of communication but also to regulations that require authorities and municipalities to ensure the rights and freedoms that people have as users of welfare services (see, for example, Montin and Granberg, 2021). The right to education, healthcare, social services and a functioning transport and energy infrastructure are just a few examples of these. At the same time, there are specific laws, rules and regulations within public organizations that form the basis for their functioning as democratic organizations. Such rules and regulations include areas such as workplace participation, discrimination, equal treatment, transparency and corruption.

Our study is not primarily about whether Swedish authorities and municipalities came to strengthen or restrict democratic elements in and around their organizations. That will be a theme for future research projects. But we must at least touch briefly on these questions, especially when parts of our material indicate that the way in which people and their organizations within the public sector handled the pandemic had both clear and more indirect effects on democratic processes that are usually taken for granted – both in this sector and more generally. Admittedly, there is support in law for some of the democratic rights/obligations to be limited or overridden in serious crises and extraordinary events. But on the whole, the foundations of a democratically functioning public sector must be maintained even in these situations (Hirschfeldt and Petersson, 2020).

More than the 'formal' restriction of democratic foundations of the governance and organization of the public sector, we want to use our concept of pandemic democracy to point to aspects that concern the adjustments and limitations in work tasks, work routines and relationships that arose in the operational management of the pandemic and implied adaptations in which staff at government agencies and municipal organizations sought solutions for how best to respond to the risks and challenges that COVID-19 posed to their work.

The first aspect of how local democracy came to be challenged relates to the development we described earlier. This development suggests that there were changes in the relationships between the governing body (for example the municipal chair) and the elected representatives (for example, the municipal council) and their approaches to the pandemic, with the former being given a greater, and sometimes unanchored, mandate to implement necessary changes and adaptations in the governance and organization of municipalities and authorities. We also saw that decision-making processes were assigned to people with experience in crisis management, which, in some cases, challenged the usual democratic decision-making processes. Discussions in municipal councils sometimes suffered due to the lack of technical expertise on the part of senior members, leaving more room for decision making outside the framework of these assemblies. In other cases, municipal officials could make decisions with little support on certain (democratically) central functions and processes without much discussion, transparency or scrutiny, such as, for example, when municipal refugee reception centres or government service centres wanted to limit their availability and capacity.

Welfare professionals' limitations, and their ability to maintain democratic elements in their activities, is the second aspect of the pandemic organization of the welfare sector. Again, examples from the world of schools, libraries and courts show that the democratic mission of these institutions is not self-sustaining. This mission depends to a large extent on the ability of those working in the organization of the welfare sector to translate key democratic principles into the new situations created by the pandemic. For example, continuing to lend books, organize seminars, discussions, events and author talks despite having to limit their opening hours and physical availability was one type of democratic challenge that libraries had to deal with. Being able to offer equal and equalizing teaching despite the changing circumstances of pupils and guardians made teachers think about their pedagogical approach. Ensuring legally secure and fair handling of evidence and interrogation material when it was digitized and automated posed difficult questions and dilemmas for legal professionals. Answers to the challenges faced by libraries, schools and courts were not primarily found in existing laws and regulations. Instead, it was the everyday interpretation and reinterpretation of their own pandemic-adapted work in relation to these laws and regulations that carried the democratic mission through the pandemic.

The third aspect concerns what we might call 'the internal democracy'. The transition to the pandemic way of organizing public organizations also had implications for how decisions on internal activities and priorities were made. There was a fear that remote working and digitalization would lead to a lack of discussion, limited space for the exchange of ideas and experiences and a lack of feedback. This lack of opportunities to participate in the internal work of government agencies and municipal organizations was also reinforced during periods of high risk of infection by a fear of physically participating in meetings, reviews and coffee breaks.

These and similar occasions were considered important to maintain the feeling of being part of the welfare activities where decisions would be made in dialogue and consensus. Most people expressed concern about how the return to 'normal' would take place, especially when the benefits of, for example, teleworking were perceived to greater than commitment and involvement in the future development of their own unit, group or the entire organization would be lower.

We conclude this chapter with a quote from one of our national politicians who, early in the pandemic, expressed how fragile and risky crisis management can be in terms of the foundations on which our society rests:

> Democracy is supposed to be stable and slow: proposals must be carefully considered even now, they must be prepared and submitted, but a virus has no patience. You can't negotiate with a pandemic and everything is rushed, so frustration lurks in everything we do. That's why we sleep less and try to think faster when the heat is on, using every gap in time to weigh arguments. We agree on billions to amend budgets, with quick thinking, but without blinking, we take a deep mental breath in the face of difficult questions about restricting people's freedom and end up temporarily allowing the government to close shopping malls, train stations and restaurants, reduce travel to a particular area or compulsorily buy oxygen and anaesthetics from companies. (B18, politician, Central)

Epilogue

On 5 May 2023, World Health Organization (WHO) Director-General Tedros Ghebreyesus declared the COVID-19 pandemic over. According to the WHO, the virus continues to kill and mutate, but it no longer poses a threat to public health. During the more than three-year pandemic, the virus infected 765 million people and killed 6.9 million. Europe was the continent most affected, with almost 3 million deaths due to, or as a result of, the infection.

In Sweden, life had already transitioned to a post-pandemic state in the late spring of 2022. The period since then has passed since then has offered numerous evaluations, reflections and reviews of how the pandemic was handled in different areas and what consequences it had. At the same time, media coverage, and thus public interest in the pandemic, has waned. The outbreak of war in Ukraine in the spring of 2022 and the subsequent economic developments, with increased inflation, galloping energy prices and rising interest rates, have quickly taken over the media agenda. These dramatic developments have put the pandemic in a broader perspective where it has come to be regarded as a crisis that is both linked to and parallel with other existing and anticipated crises (Hole and Bakken, 2022; Lindblad, Lindqvist, Runesdotter and Wärvik, 2021). Sweden's National Audit Office pointed out just such a link in its review of the national infection control programme: 'Increased travel, climate change, zoonoses, geopolitical changes and increased migration combined with the development of both new and old infectious diseases increase the risk of global transmission' (National Audit Office, 2023/24:39).

Although the pandemic does not dominate the headlines in the daily press in the way we became accustomed to in the first two years, there has nonetheless been some news coverage in the period since. However, this has become more nuanced, and the media generally leave more room for discussions in which the pandemic is summarized and reassessed with the hindsight offered by comparative data and statistics from other countries. The latest reports on the impact of the pandemic on Swedish society have sought to respond to the criticism of the 'strategy' that many attributed to the Public Health Agency of Sweden and the Swedish government and the public sector's decentralized organization, which in many ways has been identified as responsible for the almost 20,000 COVID-related deaths registered by the Public Health Agency up to and including June 2023.

In the spring of 2020, Sweden was singled out by many international organizations and national critics as an irresponsible country that refused to impose a general lockdown, choosing instead to go its own way with recommendations and an organization of welfare that was based on keeping most public services open for as long as possible. Open schools became the symbol of 'the Swedish strategy'. Three years later, when the excess mortality for various European countries could be compared by Statistics Sweden, it became clear that Sweden had the lowest excess mortality during the pandemic years compared to the years 2017–2019. In Sweden, excess mortality increased by only 4.4 per cent, in contrast to countries in Eastern and Southern Europe, which had excess mortality rates close to or above 15 per cent during the same period (Haglund, 2023).

In their book *Did Lockdowns Work? The Verdict on Covid Restrictions*, published by the Institute of Economic Affairs in London, economists Lars Jonung and colleagues analysed 19,000 studies on the management of the pandemic and its societal effects and concluded that the legally enforced lockdowns had no significant impact on excess mortality. However, lockdowns had significant economic, social and political costs. Jonung and colleagues also pointed out that 'countries with more severe lockdowns did not exhibit noticeably lower excess mortality than countries like Sweden with less lockdowns' (Kjällkvist, 2023).

Thus, the spring of 2023 became a time of international vindication for Anders Tegnell, who resigned as state epidemiologist. In an interview in *Svenska Dagbladet* under the heading 'Anders Tegnell doesn't like the word "revenge"', Tegnell, who was officially responsible for most of the measures applied during the pandemic, protested against the use of the word 'revenge' and played down the use of 'excess mortality' as the measure that would give us the full answer to how countries were dealing with the pandemic. However, Tegnell's statement confirms rather than contradicts the accuracy of the wording (Bergstedt, 2023).

But not all the comments made in the spring of 2023 were positive. The WHO Director-General, while declaring the end of the pandemic, was also clear that many of the mistakes made by countries in their pandemic management could have been avoided. Above all, he pointed to shortcomings and mistakes in the organization and coordination of various efforts, including the dissemination of information, the use of face masks and vaccination. He also highlighted increased inequality and reduced solidarity as aspects that the countries did not manage very well during the pandemic. Sweden was no exception in this regard.

The review of national infection control in Sweden appeared to reach a similar conclusion to the WHO. Despite acknowledging that 'infection control is a complex area: what is an effective way of dealing with an outbreak of infectious disease in one situation may prove ineffective in another', the National Audit Office's reviewers concluded that the organization of infection control in Sweden suffered from a lack of efficiency and clarity of governance (The Swedish National Audit Office, 2023: 4). It was noted that these deficiencies were mainly due to fragmentation of responsibility and insufficient coordination between the Public Health Agency and the different regions, counties and municipalities. According to the National Audit Office, the Swedish arrangement, which is based on the delegation of responsibility according to the principle of proximity, works well in normal public health interventions but entails a higher risk of ineffective management in the event of the large-scale spread of infection. The review concluded that changes in the organization of welfare provision, not least in the context of public health, are needed in order to be better prepared for future and pandemics. And as the new Director-General of the Public Health Agency of Sweden, Karin Tegmark Wisell (2023), wrote in an opinion piece in *Dagens Nyheter* on 13 May 2023, there are some organizational efforts to be made to increase resilience in the face of new pandemics.

Is there anything in the stories, reasoning and thoughts presented in this book that can help the future planning and organization of the welfare sector? What would be a message to responsible politicians, management staff and various welfare professions so that they can strengthen their preparedness and resilience for future crises – both those as yet unknown and those already looming on the horizon? Underestimating the reader's ability to find answers to the questions with which we began the book risks limiting the discussions that we hope this book has the potential to invite.

Instead, we want to follow the example of French sociologist Bruno Latour and invite discussion of the way the pandemic has been managed as part of an ongoing transformation of the public sector. From the very start of the pandemic, Latour (2021) saw that environmentally destructive industrial production and thus also large parts of the world's economic system could be both paused and redirected. This is an outstanding achievement in itself, considering how unshakable and important this system is considered to be for the continued growth and development of the economy and society (Dahl et al, 2023).

However, if the pandemic enabled political decision makers and countries' populations to imagine and accept far-reaching restrictions on individual and national rights and freedoms and economic prosperity, what are they and we prepared to give up when mankind faces crises that threaten our very existence? Latour believed that the global willingness to sacrifice and change in the management of the pandemic could not be translated into real policy proposals to address the environmental and climate crisis. He suggested that we should use our own experience to determine what assets we are willing to give up and what measures we are prepared to take if we are to have a reasonable chance of overcoming this crisis and future crises. It is at the intersection of our responses that we can look for real political expressions of possible ways forward, said Latour.

If we translate Latour's thought experiment to the ability of the Swedish public sector to deal with current and future crises, what experiences and lessons should we draw on? In addition to the issue of climate change, this sector faces the need to solve serious challenges in areas such as education, migration, segregation, integration, organized crime, changing demographics, knowledge resistance, corruption, political populism and many other parallel and related crises. The stories and illustrations in this book can be read as expressing both individual and collective responses to the questions Latour would like us to ask in relation to the various crises: what is the public sector attached to? What are we – its users, carriers, critics and defenders – ready to give up? Which relationships, principles and values are we ready to continue developing, and which have we already decided to dismantle? Organizational researchers tend to link the answers to these questions to areas that we are used to thinking about: leadership and formal organization (which during the pandemic seemed to be both challenged and strengthened); ideas on external governance that challenge context-specific and situation-specific professional knowledge; the importance of collegiality in welfare production (that is, the transfer of knowledge and skills between professions and people closest to the core mission of the authorities and municipalities); the role of digital tools in monitoring and interfering with the personal integrity of public employees, users of welfare services and people in general.

However, our reading is not the only one possible, and it should be related to alternative readings and starting points. Here, the interested reader, the welfare politician, the operations manager and the practitioners of the professions and occupations that are central to the ability of our authorities and municipalities to continue to deliver on the social mission they have been given must step forward and make their own reading and interpretation.

APPENDIX 1

Commentaries on Method for Chapters 9 and 10

Commentary on Method – Chapter 9

Signe Jernberg

Chapter 9 is based on material collected partly through interviews and partly through a specific content analysis. This content analysis covers articles in the Swedish press related to libraries and the COVID-19 pandemic during the period from 1 February 2020 to 28 February 2022. The period is intended to capture the time from the beginning of the COVID outbreak up to a few weeks after the final restrictions were lifted on 9 February 2022. The following search terms were used in the search: Library* AND (corona OR COVID* OR restrictions OR recommendations OR sars-cov* OR pandemic).

The search results were manually reviewed to ensure that the articles addressed changes in library operations due to the COVID-19 pandemic. Both news articles and opinion pieces were collected, but only the former are included in the current analysis. The figures we presented in Chapter 9 show the number of articles per month in the selection, as well as the number of analyses and opinion pieces.

After the data collection was complete, we coded the texts to answer questions about what changes were made, why the changes were made and who spoke about the changes. The basic coding structure is derived from the five classic elements that 'should' be included in a news article: what, who, when, where and why. We reviewed a selection of articles to find keywords that answer these questions. We then used these keywords to search for and automatically code words in all articles in the selection.

The keywords were grouped into the following categories and listed under each question:

What has been done?

- Activities at the libraries (such as book clubs, language cafés, short story contests, readings);
- opening hours (changed opening hours, closures, decisions to remain open despite restrictions, reopening after closure);
- support and accessibility (such as phone support, IT courses);
- loans (such as book drops, e-media, changes in loan regulations);
- distribution of books (such as take-away loans, home delivery);
- measures in the premises (such as spaced-out seating, fewer study spots, self-service, plexiglass).

Why have the changes been made, that is, what was the motivation behind the changes?

- The library's democratic and societal mission (for example, to promote access to reliable information, because libraries are a statutory activity, or to ensure that even high-risk groups have access to literature. These motivations are linked to the formulations in The Swedish Library Act (2013:801) and The Library Law (2013:801) that libraries should promote free expression and foster the status of literature and interest in education, among others);
- staff safety (to reduce the risk of staff getting infected);
- due to COVID/to reduce the spread (general statements that changes are made 'due to COVID', 'to reduce the spread', to 'avoid gatherings' and so on);
- referring to authorities' recommendations/restrictions;
- staffing (that is, staff shortage due to illness or childcare).

Who speaks in the article?

- librarian;
- library, cultural or leisure manager;
- communications manager;
- municipal director;
- chair of the Municipal Executive Board;
- chairs of various committees.

* The presence of a category, for example 'distribution of books', is counted once per article regardless of how many times it is mentioned overall, to make the data as comparable as possible across the entire dataset.

Commentary on Method – Chapter 10

Charlotta Kronblad

Research on the digital transformation in the courts during the pandemic can naturally take many different forms. To find out how the courts acted during the pandemic, and what this entailed, we could choose to delve into a specific legal case and experience the changes realized in that particular case. We could also follow the work and transformation in a specific court, or on a more overarching level, collect public data on the transformation from different courts in various locations around the world. In Chapter 10, I chose to blend these approaches. I aim to convey insights based on my own experiences of the digital transformation during the pandemic, but I also want to provide a broader picture of what a digital court and a virtual trial can entail, as insights from Sweden are somewhat limited, given that the restrictions and therefore the digital transformation were much more extensive in other parts of the world. The insights I share in the chapter are thus based on a variety of sources. I have consulted books and articles that address the intersection of courts, digitalization and the pandemic on a global scale, and I also recount the stories from the research that a colleague and I conducted at a local court. Additionally, I share insights from workshops I have led at courts post-pandemic, as well as my learnings from my ongoing research on algorithmic bias. At the end of the chapter, I suggest various ways in which we can connect these different research areas and insights.

To follow and evaluate my research, it may be valuable to know that I prefer qualitative methods, which means that I am not particularly interested in quantitative data or in measuring exactly how much of the court's work was digitized during the pandemic, or how many virtual trials were held. Instead, I am interested in understanding what changed and what this shift means in the long run.

APPENDIX 2

Details of Field Work

Table A.1: Locations of interviews

Municipality	Number of interviews
North	6
West	15
West South	12
Central East	13
Central	8
South Central	15
South East	3
Central North	1
North Central	2
	75

Table A.2: Interviewees by profession and municipality

Profession and municipality	Year
B1, assistant nurse, Central East	2020
B2, food inspector, Central	2020
B3, military officer, West South	2020
B4, researcher, Central	2020
B5, teacher, West South	2020
B6, teacher, West South	2020
B7, nurse, Central East	2020
B8, art teacher1, West South	2020
B9, line manager, West South	2020
B10, social secretary, Central	2020

Table A.2: Interviewees by profession and municipality (continued)

Profession and municipality	Year
B11, social service coordinator, West South	2020
B12, university administrator, Central East	2020
B13, information counsellor, West South	2020
B14, university lecturer, Central	2020
B15, communication specialist, West South	2020
B16, art teacher2, West South	2020
B17, business coordinator, Central	2020
B18, politician, Central	2020
B19, museum line manager, West South	2020
B20, employment officer, Central North	2020
B21, researcher1, Central East	2020
B22, researcher2, Central East	2020
B23, teacher, Central East	2020
B24, asylum officer, Central	2020
B25, healthcare project manager, Central East	2020
B26, personnel manager, Central East	2020
B27, information advisor, Centre	2020
B28, nurse, Central East	2020
B29, family counsellor, Central East	2020
B30, education manager, Central	2020
B31, deputy director of healthcare, Central East	2020
B32, head of office, Central East	2020
C1, social secretary, North	2021
C2, municipal board secretary, West	2021
C3, municipal secretary, North	2021
C4, environmental inspector, North	2021
C5, administrator, North	2021
C6, environment manager, North	2021
C7, environmental and health protection inspector, West	2021
C8, principal, West	2021
C9, IT manager, West	2021
C10, library coordinator, West	2021
C11, training manager, West	2021
C12, public health coordinator, West	2021

(continued)

Table A.2: Interviewees by profession and municipality (continued)

Profession and municipality	**Year**
C13, teacher, West	2021
C14, building inspector, West	2021
C15, university administrator, Central East	2021
C16, primary school teacher, West	2021
C17, teacher, West	2021
C18, teacher, Central East	2021
C19, municipal manager, West	2021
C20, local government chairman, West	2021
C21, municipal secretary, West	2021
C22, home economics teacher, West	2021
D1, teacher, Central	2021
D2, administrator, children and education, South Central	2022
D3, library coordinator, South Central	2022
D4, social secretary, Central South	2022
D5, library assistant, South Central	2022
D6, technical director, South Central	2022
D7, social services manager, Central South	2022
D8, economist, South Central	2022
D9, administrative assistant, Central South	2022
D10, social worker, South Central	2022
D11, municipal director, Central South	2022
D12, counsellor, South Central	2022
D13, social secretary, South Central	2022
D14, head teacher, East Central	2022
D15, principal, South Central	2022
D16, head of administration, South Central	2022
D17, teacher, South West	2022
D18, youth leader, South East	2022
D19, youth worker, South Central	2022
D20, deputy municipal director, Central North	2022
D21, receptionist, North Central	2022

Notes

Chapter 1

[1] Foreword to *På liv och död: berättelser från en pandemi* (Kommunal, 2020).

[2] This scientific production also includes texts that used Sweden as comparison or as a reference point.

[3] In Czarniawska et al (2022: 21–47).

Chapter 2

[1] A series of reports from Kommunforskning i Västsverige on how municipalities and cities have dealt with the COVID-19 pandemic is available from: www.kfi.se [Accessed 15 March 2022].

Chapter 3

[1] See 'Nytt coronavirus upptäckt i Kina' (New coronavirus discovered in China) on the Public Health Agency of Sweden website. Available from: https://www.folkhalsomyndigheten.se/nyheter-och-press/nyhetsarkiv/2020/januari/nytt-coronavirus-upptackt-i-kina/ [Accessed 15 March 2022].

[2] From the Public Health Agency of Sweden website, press release in January 2020 'Sverige har en stark smittskyddsorganisation' (Sweden has a strong infectious disease control organization). Available from: https://www.folkhalsomyndigheten.se/nyheter-och-press/nyhetsarkiv/2020/januari/sverige-har-en-stark-smittskyddsorganisation/ [Accessed 15 March 2022].

[3] From Scandinavian Airlines press office. Available from: https://infoexpress.se/information-regarding-sas-flights-to-and-from-china/ [Accessed 15 March 2022].

[4] From the government press release issued in March 2020. Available from: https://www.regeringen.se/pressmeddelanden/2020/03/ [Accessed 15 March 2022].

[5] From the Public Health Agency of Sweden website, press release in February 2020 'Ingen spridning av coronavirus i Sverige' (No spread of coronavirus in Sweden). Available from: https://www.folkhalsomyndigheten.se/nyheter-och-press/nyhetsarkiv/2020/februari/ingen-spridning-av-coronavirus-i-sverige/ [Accessed 15 March 2022].

[6] From the World Health Organization (WHO) website, opening remarks of the Director-General at the media briefing on COVID-19 on 11 March 2020. Available from: https://www.who.int/director-general/speeches/detail/who-director-general-s-opening-remarks-at-the-media-briefing-on-Covid-19 [Accessed 15 March 2022].

[7] From the news section of the state website on crisis information. Available from: https://www.krisinformation.se/nyheter/2020/mars/ [Accessed 15 March 2022].

[8] From the news on the Public Health Agency of Sweden website. Available from: https://www.folkhalsomyndigheten.se/nyheter-och-press/nyhetsarkiv/2020/mars/presstraff-om-den-nationella-pandemigruppens-mote/ [Accessed 15 March 2022].

[9] 'On March 11, 2020, the World Health Organization (WHO) declared the Covid-19 outbreak a global pandemic, and shortly after, the well-organized, orderly and lean Personal Protective Equipment (PPE) supply chain reached a tipping point. Chaos broke loose; demand skyrocketed' (Soelberg, 2022: 136).

[10] Trade union for municipal workers.

[11] From the website of Ljusdal municipality. Available from: https://www.ljusdal.se/ [Accessed 15 March 2022].

Chapter 4

[1] From the WHO Director-General's speech at the security conference in Munich in February 2020. Available from: https://www.who.int/director-general/speeches/detail/munich-security-conference [Accessed 20 March 2022].

Chapter 6

[1] From Public Health Agency of Sweden website, news on a study on the mental health consequences of COVID-19. Available from: https://www.folkhalsomyndigheten.se/livsvillkor-levnadsvanor/psykisk-halsa-och-suicidprevention/psykisk-halsa/covid-19-och-psykisk-halsa/covid-19-pandemin-och-befolkningens-psykiska-halsa/ [Accessed 20 March 2022].

[2] From Public Health Agency of Sweden website, news on a report on the effects of COVID-19 on public health. Available from: https://www.folkhalsomyndigheten.se/publikationer-och-material/publikationsarkiv/s/sa-paverkade-covid-19-pandemin-folkhalsan-under-2020/ [Accessed 20 March 2022].

Chapter 12

[1] This term fuses 'pandemic' with '-cracy', from the Greek *kratos*, meaning strength, power, force, firmness.

References

Agevall, Ola and Olofsson, Gunnar (2020) 'Administratörerna: administration, kontroll och styrning vid svenska universitet och högskolor', *Arkiv. Tidskrift för samhällsanalys*, (12): 7–59.

Ahlbäck Öberg, Shirin and Bringselius, Louise (2015) 'Professionalism and organizational performance in the wake of new managerialism', *European Political Science Review*, 7(4): 499–523.

Ahlbäck Öberg, Shitin, Bull, Thomas, Hasselberg, Ylva and Stenlås, Niclas (2016) 'Professions under siege', *Statsvetenskaplig tidskrift*, 118(1): 93–126.

Ahrne, Göran and Papakostas, Apostolis (2002) *Organisationer, samhälle och globalisering*, Lund: Studentlitteratur.

AJUFE (2022) 'The Brazilian judiciary and COVID 19', Available from: https://www.ajufe.org.br/imprensa/artigos/14801-the-brazilian-judiciary-and [Accessed 15 June 2024].

Alvehus, Johan and Loodin, Henrik (2020) 'Making sense of institutional changes in the welfare professions', *Scandinavian Journal of Public Administration*, 24(2): 65–7.

Askim, J. and Bergström, T. (2022) 'Between lockdown and calm down: Comparing the COVID-19 responses of Norway and Sweden', *Local Government Studies*, 48(2): 291–311.

Aucante, Yohann (2022) *The Swedish Experiment: The COVID-19 Response and its* Covid-19 [Accessed 29 November 2022].

Alvinius, Aida and Starrin, Bengt (2022) 'Hotet mot det sociala självet till följd av Covid-19 pandemin: en sonderande analys', *Arbetsmarknad & Arbetsliv*, 28(3–4): 67–86.

Anderberg, Johan (2021) *Flocken: berättelsen om hur Sverige valde väg under pandemin*, Stockholm: Albert Bonniers förlag.

Bergdahl, Nina and Jalal, Nouri (2021) 'COVID-19 and crisis-prompted distance education in Sweden', *Technology, Knowledge and Learning*, 26(3): 443–59.

Bergmann, Sigurd and Lindström, Martin (2023) *Sweden's Pandemic Experiment*, Milton Park: Taylor & Francis.

Bergstedt, Therese (2023) 'Anders Tegnell: "Gillar inte ordet 'revansch'", Available from: https://www.svd.se/a/JQvVnj/anders-tegnell-efter-pandemin-overdodlighet-ger-inte-hela-svaret [Accessed 16 June 2023].

Björkdahl, Joakim and Kronblad, Charlotta (2021) 'Getting on track for digital work: digital transformation in an administrative court before and during COVID-19', *Journal of Professions and Organization*, 8(3): 374–93.

Blomgren, Maria and Waks, Caroline (2017) 'The impact of institutional pluralism on governmental reforms in the public sector', *Scandinavian Journal of Public Administration*, 21(4): 3–25.

Bornemark, Jonna (2018) 'The limits of ratio: An analysis of NPM in Sweden using Nicholas of Cusa's understanding of reason', in Ajana Btihaj (ed.) *Metric Culture*, Bingley: Emerald Publishing Limited, 235–53.

Bornemark, Jonna (2020) *Horisonten finns alltid kvar: om det bortglömda omdömet*, Stockholm: Volante.

Borraz, Olivier and Jacobsson, Bengt (2023) 'Organizing expertise during a crisis: France and Sweden in the fight against COVID-19', *Journal of Organizational Sociology*, 1(1): 73–101.

Boström, Lena and Rising Holmström, Malin (2023) 'Students' experience of uncertain times: learning and well-being in Swedish upper secondary schools during the pandemic', *Social Sciences & Humanities Open*, 7(1): 100489.

Bringselius, Louise (2017) *Tillitsbaserad styrning och ledning: Ett ramverk*, Lund: Tillitdelegationen.

Brorström, Björn and Löfström, Mikael (2022) 'Regioner och kommuner har bestått provet-om hanteringen av konsekvenserna av coronapandemin', *Nordisk Administrativt Tidskrift*, 99(2): 1–17.

Browning, Larry D., Sørnes, Jan-Oddvar and Svenkerud, Peer Jacob (2022) 'Organizational communication and technology in the time of coronavirus: ethnographies from the first year of the pandemic', in Larry D. Browning, Jan-Oddvar Sørnes and Peer Jacob Svenkerud (eds) *Organizational Communication and Technology in the Time of Coronavirus*, London: Palgrave Macmillan, 1–17.

Brynjolfsson, Erik and McAfee, Andrew (2016) *The second machine age*. W.W. Norton.

Cameron, Iain and Jonsson-Cornell, Anna (2022) 'Dealing with COVID-19 in Sweden: Choosing a different path', in Grogan, Joelle and Donald, Alice (eds) *Routledge Handbook of Law and the COVID-19 Pandemic*, London: Routledge, 237–47.

Carlsson, Fredrik, Iacobaeus, Helena and Wihlborg, Elin (2021) 'Demokratiska beslut i coronatider: digitala verktyg för att ställa om snarare än ställa in', *Statsvetenskaplig tidskrift*, 123(5): 431–49.

Czarniawska, Barbara, Pallas, Josef and Raviola, Elena (2022) 'Pandemicracy and organizing in unsettling times', in Larry D. Browning, Jan-Oddvar Sørnes and Peer Jacob Svenkerud (eds) *Organizational Communication and Technology in Time of Coronavirus*, London: Palgrave Macmillan, 21–48.

Corona Commission (2020:09) Kommittéberättelse. Available from: https://www.riksdagen.se/sv/dokument-och-lagar/dokument/kommitteberattelse/coronakommissionen-s-202009_h8b2s09/ [Accessed 23 September 2024].

Dahl, Matilda, Helin, Jenny and Ubbe, Elisabeth (2023) *Hemkomstens ekonomi: Företagande bortom erövring*, Lund: Studentlitteratur AB.

De', Rahul, Pandey, Neena and Pal, Abhipsa (2020) 'Impact of digital surge during COVID-19 pandemic: a viewpoint on research and practice', *International Journal of Information Management*, 55: 102–71.

Dimond, Rebecca (2021) 'On "being there": a rejoinder to "Collecting qualitative data during a pandemic" by David Silverman', *Communication & Medicine*, 17(2): 173–6.

Einhorn, Lena (2022) *Bland hobbyepidemiologer och expertmyndigheter: en resa i pandemins Sverige*, Stockholm: Nordstedts förlag.

Engström, Lisa (2020) 'Främjar bibliotek verkligen demokrati?', *Bibliotek i samhälle*, 1: 31.

Engwall, Kristina and Storm, Palle (2021) 'The importance of keeping a social perspective during pandemic times: social psychiatry in Sweden', *International Social Work*, 64(5): 745–9.

Eriksson, Charlotta and Ivarsson Westerberg, Anders (2021) Ingen reklam tack: en ESO-rapport om myndigheternas kommunikation. Available from: https://eso.expertgrupp.se/wp-content/uploads/2020/06/ESO-2021_3-Ingen-reklam-tack_webb.pdf [Accessed 23 September 2024].

Eriksson, Thord (2020) 'Fel att nämna bibliotek i samma mening som badhus', Available from: https://www.biblioteksbladet.se/nyheter/fel-att-namna-bibliotek-i-samma-mening-som-badhus/ [Accessed 9 June 2023].

Eriksson-Zetterquist, Ulla and Pallas, Josef (2022) 'Bureaucracy under pressure: new(s) management practices in central government agencies', *European Management Journal*, 42(3): 295–304.

Erlandsson, Sara, Ulmanen, Petra and Wittzell, Sara (2023) *COVID-19 på äldreboenden-personalens erfarenheter*, Stockholm: SNS Förlag.

Ettarh, Fobazi (2018) 'Vocational awe and librarianship: the lies we tell ourselves', *The Library with the Lead Pipe*, 10, Available from: https://www.inthelibrarywiththeleadpipe.org/2018/vocational-awe/ [Accessed 26 May 2023].

European Commission (2020) 'Vägledning från Europeiska kommissionen om användningen av reglerna om offentlig upphandling i nödsituationen i samband med COVID-19-krisen', *Europeiska unionens officiella tidning*, C108 1/1, Available from: https://eur-lex.europa.eu/legal-content/SV/TXT/PDF/?uri=CELEX:52020XC0401(05)&from=EN [Accessed 1 April 2020].

Fernemark, Hanna, Skagerström, Janna, Seing, Ida, Hårdstedt, Maria, Schildmeijer, Kristina and Nilsen, Per (2022) 'Working conditions in primary healthcare during the COVID-19 pandemic: an interview study with physicians in Sweden', *BMJ Open*, 12(2): e055035.

Forssell, Anders and Westerberg Ivarsson, Anders (2014) *Administrationssamhället*, Lund: Studentlitteratur.

Fredriksson, Magnus and Pallas, Josef (2020) 'Public sector communication and mediatization', in Luoma-aho, Vilma and Canel, María-José (eds) *The Handbook of Public Sector Communication*, New York: Wiley & Sons, 167–79.

Ghersetti, Marina and Odén, Tomas (2021) 'Coronapandemin våren 2020: en undersökning av nyheter och opinion', Available from: https://rib.msb.se/filer/pdf/29525.pdf [Accessed 30 April 2023].

Government Bill (2020/21:47) Following up on vaccination scheme. Available from: https://www.regeringen.se/contentassets/c552fba30d694713a047d5557f8e7336/prop.-2020_21_47.pdf [Accessed 23 September 2024].

Grafström, Maria, Qvist, Martin and Sundström, Göran (2021) *Megaprojektet Nya Karolinska Solna: Beslutsprocesserna bakom en sjukvårdsreform*, Stockholm: Makadam.

Greve, Carsten, Ejersbo, Niels, Lægreid, Per and Rykkja, Lise H. (2020) 'Unpacking Nordic administrative reforms: agile and adaptive governments', *International Journal of Public Administration*, 43(8): 697–710.

Gustafsson, Anna and Röstlund, Lisa (2019) *Konsulterna: Kampen om Karolinska*, Stockholm: Mondial.

Haglund, F. (2023) Sverige hade lägsta överdödligheten under coronapandemin i EU. *Europortalen*, 6 March 2023, Available from: https://www.europaportalen.se/2023/03/sverige-hade-lagsta-overdodligheten-under-coronapandemin-i-eu [Accessed 14 October 2024].

Hall, Patrik (2012) *Management-byråkrati*, Malmö: Liber.

Hiselius, Lena W. and Arnfalk, Peter (2021) 'When the impossible becomes possible: COVID-19's impact on work and travel patterns in Swedish public agencies', *European Transport Research Review*, 13(1): 1–10.

Hirschfeldt, Johan and Petersson, Olof (2020) *Rättsregler i kris*, Stockholm: Dialogos.

Hole, Åse Storhaug and Bakken, Bjørn Tallak (2022) 'The impact of trust in time of COVID-19: trust in crisis management and crisis communication in Inland Norway University of Applied Sciences', in Larry Browning, Jan-Oddvar Sørnes and Peer Jacob Svenkerud (eds) *Organizational Communication and Technology in Time of Coronavirus*, London: Palgrave Macmillan, 251–76.

Huupponen, Maru (2020) An der Corona-Front. Available from: https://library.fes.de/pdf-files/bueros/stockholm/18223.pdf [Accessed 23 September 2024].

Jacobsson, Bengt (2020) 'Pandemi och politik: några missförstånd', *Organisation & Samhälle*, 2: 4–9.

Jacobsson, Kerstin, Wallinder, Ylva and Seing, Ida (2020) 'Street-level bureaucrats under new managerialism: a comparative study of agency cultures and caseworker role identities in two welfare state bureaucracies', *Journal of Professions and Organization*, 7(3): 316–33.

Jansson, Anna and Parding, Karolina (2011) 'Changed governance of public sector organisations: challenged conditions for intra-professional relations?', *International Journal of Public Sector Management*, 24(3): 177–86.

Jernberg, Signe and Pallas, Josef (2022) 'Under the press(ure)? The role of media in organization and provision of municipal elderly care', *Scandinavian Journal of Management*, 26(2): 67–88.

Källkvist, Peter (2023) 'Nedstängningar under pandemin sannolikt det största policymisstaget i modern tid', Available from: https://www.lu.se/artikel/nedstangningar-under-pandemin-sannolikt-det-storsta-policymisstaget-i-modern-tid?ref=pressrelease [Accessed 16 June 2023].

Kjellgren, Thomas, Kristofersson, Tuija Nieminen and Nilsson, Per (2020) 'När samhället krisar behövs biblioteken som mest', Available from: https://www.sydostran.se/insandare/nar-samhallet-krisar-behovs-biblioteken-som-mest/ [Accessed 9 June 2023].

Kranich, Nancy C. (2001) 'Libraries, the internet and democracy', in Nancy Kranich (ed) *Libraries and Democracy: The Cornerstones of Liberty*, Chicago: American Library Association, 83–95.

Kranich, Nancy C. (2020) 'Libraries and democracy revisited', *The Library Quarterly*, 90(2): 121–53.

Kreitz-Sandberg, Susanne, Ringer, Nils and Fredriksson, Ulf (2022) '"We have our lessons in Teams": strategies chosen in Swedish schools during the COVID-19 pandemic and consequences for students in upper secondary education', *Tertium Comparationis Journal für International und Interkulturell Vergleichende Erziehungswissenschaft*, 28(3): 250–73.

Kronblad, Charlotte (2021) 'Digital transformation of the legal field: a bubble in trouble', PhD thesis, Gothenburg: Chalmers Tekniska Högskola.

Kronblad, Charlotte and Pregmark, Johanna (2021) 'How COVID-19 has changed the digital trajectory for professional advisory firms', in Jungwoo Lee and Spring H. Han (eds) *The Future of Service Post-COVID-19 Pandemic*, Singapore: Springer, 101–21.

Kuhlmann, Sabine, Hellström, Mikael, Ramberg, Ulf and Reiter, Renate (2021) 'Tracing divergence in crisis governance: responses to the COVID-19 pandemic in France, Germany and Sweden compared', *International Review of Administrative Sciences*, 87(3): 556–75.

Lægreid, Per and Verhoest, Koen (2010) *Governance of Public Sector Organizations: Proliferation, Autonomy and Performance*, London: Palgrave Macmillan.

Latour, Bruno (2021) *After Lockdown: A Metamorphosis*, Cambridge: Polity Press.

Lee, Helena (2021) 'Changes in workplaces during the COVID-19 pandemic: the roles of emotion, psychological safety, and organisation support', *Journal of Organizational Effectiveness: People and Performance*, 8(1): 97–128.

Lidegran, Ida, Hultqvist, Elisabeth, Bertilsson, Emil and Börjesson, Mikael (2021) 'Insecurity, lack of support, and frustration: a sociological analysis of how three groups of students reflect on their distance education during the pandemic in Sweden', *European Journal of Education*, 56(4): 550–63.

Lind, Linda Ekström, Bylund, Anna Martín and Stenliden, Linnéa (2021) 'COVID-19 i svenska skolor synliggör sårbarhetens potential i lärares praktik', *Atena didaktik*, 3(2), Available from: https://doi.org/10.3384/atena.2020.3345 [Accessed 18 November 2020].

Lindblad, Sverker, Lindqvist, Anders, Runesdotter, Caroline and Wärvik, Gunn-Britt (2021) 'In education we trust: on handling the COVID-19 pandemic in the Swedish welfare state', *Zeitschrift für Erziehungswissenschaft*, 24(2): 503–19.

Lundberg, Susanna (2021) 'Rekrytera och behålla personal i den kommunala äldreomsorgen under COVID-19', *Socialvetenskaplig tidskrift*, 28(4): 477–97.

Lyrstrand Larssen, Hellen (2020) 'Ingen anledning till oro, menar läkare', *Kungälv-Posten*, 31 January.

Martinsson, Eva, Garmy, Pernilla and Einberg, Eva-Lena (2021) 'School nurses' experience of working in school health service during the COVID-19 pandemic in Sweden', *International Journal of Environmental Research and Public Health*, 18(13): 6713.

Meagher, Gabrielle and Szebehely, Marta (2019) 'The politics of profit in Swedish welfare services: four decades of social democratic ambivalence', *Critical Social Policy*, 39(3): 455–76.

Montin, Stig and Granberg, Mikael (2021) 'Corona, krishantering och demokrati: om meddelarfrihet vid en extraordinär händelse', *Statsvetenskaplig tidskrift*, 123(5): 407–28.

Mounk, Yascha (2018) *The People vs Democracy: Why Our Freedom Is in Danger and How to Save It*, Cambridge, MA: Harvard University Press.

National Audit Office (2023) Riksrevisionens rapport om det nationella smittskyddet, 2023/24:39. Regeringskansliet. Available from: https://www.regeringen.se/contentassets/246a3ff5380c4c899bdb30aed2060d51/skr.232403900webb-002.pdf [Accessed 14 October 2024].

National Board of Health and Welfare (2022) E-hälsa och välfärdsteknik I kommunerna 2022. Available from: https://www.socialstyrelsen.se/globalassets/sharepoint-dokument/artikelkatalog/ovrigt/2022-5-7897.pdf [Accessed 23 September 2024].

Nilsberth, Maria, Liljekvist, Yvonne, Olin-Scheller, Christina, Samuelsson, Johan and Hallquist, Claes (2021) 'Digital teaching as the new normal? Swedish upper secondary teachers' experiences of emergency remote teaching during the COVID-19 crisis', *European Educational Research Journal*, 20(4): 442–62.

Novus rapport (2018) 'Svensk biblioteksförening', Available from: https://wwwbiblioteksfor.cdn.triggerfish.cloud/uploads/2018/05/novus-rapport-svensk-biblioteksforening-final.pdf [Accessed 26 May 2023].

Öckert, Björn (2021) 'Frånvaro i skolan under coronapandemin: hur kan resultaten komma att påverkas', in Anna Sjögren (ed) *Barn och unga under coronapandemin: lärdomar från forskning om uppväxtmiljö, skolgång, utbildning, och arbetsmarknadsinträde*, Uppsala: IFAU, 33–64.

Ödlund, Ann (2010) 'Pulling the same way? A multi-perspective study of crisis cooperation in government', *Journal of Contingencies and Crisis Management*, 18: 96–107.

Plenty, Stephanie, Bracegirdle, Chloe, Dollman, Jörg and Spiegler, Olivia (2021) 'Changes in young adults' mental well-being before and during the early stage of the COVID-19 pandemic: disparities between ethnic groups in Germany', *Child and Adolescent Psychiatry and Mental Health*, 15(69), Available from: https://doi.org/10.1186/s13034-021-00418-x [Accessed 13 April 2022].

Popowich, Sam (2019) *Confronting the Democratic Discourse of Librarianship: A Marxist Approach*, Sacramento, CA: Library Juice Press.

Public Health Agency (2020a) Nytt coronavirus upptäckt I Kina. Available from: https://www.folkhalsomyndigheten.se/nyheter-och-press/nyhetsarkiv/2020/januari/nytt-coronavirus-upptackt-i-kina/ [Accessed 13 April 2022].

Public Health Agency (2020b) Förekomsten av covid-19 i Sverige 21–24 april och 25–28 maj 2020. Available from: https://www.folkhalsomyndigheten.se/contentassets/fb47e03453554372ba75ca3d3a6ba1e7/forekomstren-covid-19-sverige-21-24-april-25-28-maj-2020.pdf [Accessed 23 September 2024].

Public Health Agency (2020c) Covid-19 Pandemic and the population's mental health. Available from: https://www.folkhalsomyndigheten.se/publikationer-och-material/publikationsarkiv/c/covid-19-pandemin-och-befolkningens-psykiska-halsa--vad-indikerar-longitudinella-studier [Accessed 13 April 2022].

Public Health Agency (2021d) Så påverkade covid-19 folkhälsan under 2020. Available from: https://www.folkhalsomyndigheten.se/contentassets/378883b7e63547179491433be2ff11f6/sa-paverkade-covid-19-pandemin-folkhalsan-2020.pdf [Accessed 13 April 2020].

Ranemo, Cecilia (2020) 'Bibliotek 2020: offentligt finansierade bibliotek', Available from: https://www.mynewsdesk.com/se/kungliga_biblioteket/pressreleases/biblioteksstatistiken-2020-oekad-utlaaning-av-e-boecker-under-pandemins-foersta-aar-3100358 [Accessed 13 April 2022].

Regeringsformen (1974:152) Kungörelse (1974:152) om beslutad ny regeringsform. Swedish law about form of governement. Available from: https://www.riksdagen.se/sv/dokument-och-lagar/dokument/svensk-forfattningssamling/kungorelse-1974152-om-beslutad-ny-regeringsform_sfs-1974-152/ [Accessed 23 September 2024].

Swedish Library Act (2013:801) 'Kulturdepartementet', Available from: https://www.riksdagen.se/sv/dokument-lagar/dokument/svensk-forfattningssamling/bibliotekslag-2013801_sfs-2013-801 [Accessed 26 May 2023].

Siebert, Sabina (2020) 'Symbolic demarcation: the role of status symbols in preserving interprofessional boundaries', *Journal of Professions and Organization*, 7(1): 47–69.

Social Ministry (2020) Press Conference, 22 December 2020, Available from: https://www.regeringen.se/artiklar/2020/12/vaccinering-mot-covid-19-inleds-den-27-december/ [Accessed 11 September 2024].

Soelberg, Frode (2022) 'Chaos: international sourcing of PPE and the COVID-19 pandemic', in Larry Browning, Jan-Oddvar Sørnes and Peer Jacob Svenkerud (eds) *Organizational Communication and Technology in Time of Coronavirus*, London: Palgrave Macmillan, 135–52.

Solli, Rolf, Czarniawska, Barbara, Demediuk, Peter and Anderson, Denis (2020) *Searching for New Welfare Models: Citizens' Opinions on the Past, Present and Future of the Welfare State,* New York: Springer Nature.

SOU (2021:77) Från kris till kraft. Återstart för kulturen. Available from: https://www.regeringen.se/contentassets/c96ef2e953fd481ebb68d41b980a1d0a/fran-kris-till-kraft.-aterstart-for-kulturen-sou-202177.pdf [Accessed 23 September 2024].

SOU (2021:89) Sverige under pandemin. Delbetänkande av Coronakommissionen. Available from: https://www.regeringen.se/contentassets/e1c4a1033b9042fe96c0b2a3f453ff1d/sverige-under-pandemin-volym-1_webb-1.pdf [Accessed 23 September 2024].

SOU (2022:10a) 'Sverige under pandemin, Volym 1 Samhällets, företagens och enskildas ekonomi', Slutbetänkande av Coronakommissionen.

SOU (2022:10b) 'Sverige under pandemin, Volym 2 Förutsättningar, vägval och utvärdering', Slutbetänkande av Coronakommissionen.

Sourdin, Tania, Li, Bin and McNamara, Donna (2020) 'Court innovations and access to justice in times of crisis', *Health Policy and Technology*, 9(4): 447–53.

Styhre, Alexander (2013) *Professionals Making Judgments: The Professional Skill of Valuing and Assessing*, London: Palgrave MacMillan.

Susskind, Richard (2019) *Online Courts and the Future of Justice*, Oxford: Oxford University Press.

Svensk biblioteksförening (2008) 'Bibliotekarien och professionen: en forskningsöversikt', Available from: https://wwwbiblioteksfor.cdn.triggerfish.cloud/uploads/2017/01/bibliotekarien-och-professionen.pdf [Accessed 26 May 2023].

SKR (Sveriges kommuner och regioner) (2021a) 'COVID-19 och coronaviruset: fullmäktige och nämndsammanträden', Available from: https://skr.se/skr/Covid19ochcoronaviruset/fullmaktigeochnamndsammantraden.32393.html [Accessed 9 June 2023].

SKR (Sveriges kommuner och regioner) (2021b) 'Politiska möten i kommuner och regioner under 2020', Available from: https://skr.se/download/18.583b3b0c17e40e30384485ab/1642422541298/7585-922-4.pdf [Accessed 9 June 2023].

Swedish Agency for Work Environment Expertise (2021) Rapport 2023:1. Coronapandemins konsekvenser för arbetsmiljön i Sverige (The consequences of the corona pandemic for work environment in Sweden). Available from: https://mynak.se/wp-content/uploads/2023/03/Coronapandemins-konsekvenser-for-arbetsmiljon.pdf [Accessed 10 September 2024].

Swedish Education Act (2010:800) Available from: https://www.riksdagen.se/sv/dokument-och-lagar/dokument/svensk-forfattningssamling/skollag-2010800_sfs-2010-800/ [Accessed 15 June 2024].

Tarvis, Maria, Ziegert, Kristina, Forsberg, Elenita, Andersson, Janicke and Gillsjö, Catharina (2022) 'From chaos to a new normal: the COVID-19 pandemic as experienced by municipal health and social care providers in Sweden; a qualitative study', *Nordic Journal of Nursing Research*, Available from: https://doi.org/10.1177/2057158522112 [Accessed 9 June 2023].

Tegmark Wisell, Karin (2023) 'Så måste Sverige rusta inför nästa pandemi', Available from: https://www.dn.se/debatt/sa-maste-sverige-rusta-infor-nasta-pandemi/ [Accessed 16 June 2023].

Theobald, Hildegard (2022) An der Corona-Front. Available from: https://library.fes.de/pdf-files/bueros/stockholm/17990.pdf [Accessed 23 September 2024].

Weick, Karl E. and Sutcliffe, Kathleen M. (2011) *Managing the Unexpected: Resilient Performance in an Age of Uncertainty*, New York: John Wiley & Sons.

Wolmesjö, Maria and Solli, Rolf (2021) *Framtidens välfärd-hållbar styrning, organisering och ledning*, Lund: Studentlitteratur.

Thomas, Barbro (2008) 'Från bisyssla till kulturförmedlande informations specialist: yrkesroll och arbetsvillkor i förändring', in Margareta Lundberg Rodin (ed) *Till det mänskliga ordets trygga beredskap och värn: Svensk biblioteksförening 1915–2015*, Available from: https://wwwbiblioteksfor.cdn.triggerfish.cloud/uploads/2017/01/till-det-manskliga.pdf [Accessed 26 May 2023].

Thorgersen, Ketil A. and Mars, Annette (2021) 'A pandemic as the mother of invention? Collegial online collaboration to cope with the COVID-19 pandemic', *Music Education Research*, 23(2): 225–40.

Torkelsson, Anna-Cajsa (2021) 'Utbredd psykisk ohälsa i vården efter pandemin', Available from: https://lakartidningen.se/aktuellt/nyheter/2021/12/utbredd-psykisk-ohalsa-i-varden-efter-pandemin/ [Accessed 30 April 2023].

Webley, Lisa, Flood, John, Webb, Julian, Bartlett, Francesca, Galloway, Kate and Tranter, Kieran (2019) 'The profession(s)' engagements with LawTech: narratives and archetypes of future law', *Law, Technology and Humans*, 1: 6–26.

Wiegand, Wayne A. (2015) *Part of Our Lives: A People's History of the American Public Library*, New York: Oxford University Press.

Wikforss, Åsa and Wikforss, Mårten (2021) *Därför demokrati: om kunskapen och folkstyret*, Stockholm: Fri tanke.

Willstedt, Tobias (2020) 'Från Linero till Lunds stadsbibliotek', *Bibliotek i samhälle*, 3: 14–17.

Index

References to figures appear in *italic* type.